DISPLACED

PERSON

D.A. Blyler is the author of the novel *Steffi's Club*, and an essayist whose writing has appeared in The Nation newspaper, Bangkok, among other international publications, and numerous internet journals, including Salon.com and 3am Magazine. He is also the author of two books of poetry, *Diary of a Seducer* and *Shared Solitude*.   D.A. Blyler resides in Tambon Nam Muang, Thailand.

Simon Lane is the author of four novels, *Le Veilleur*, *Still-life With Books*, *Fear*, and *Word of Mouth*. He has written for a wide variety of publications in Europe and the United States, and has worked in film, radio, and television both as a writer and an actor. Born in England, he has lived in London, Berlin, Milan, New York, and Paris. He now lives and works in Rio de Janeiro.

Marcus Reichert is an artist of various disciplines, including painting and film-making. His photographic work is represented by Michael Hoppen Contemporary, London. His filmworks are held in the Archive of the Museum of Modern Art, New York. *Reichert: The Human Edifice* by Mel Gooding, with 100 photographs by the artist in colour, is published by Artmedia Press, London.

DISPLACED
PERSON

Poetry, Pornography & Politics

Selected Writings 1970-2005
MARCUS REICHERT

Z I G G U R A T   B O O K S
PSI Publishing, St. Quentin House, Fitzhugh Grove,
London SW18 3SE

ACKNOWLEDGMENTS

Thanks to Rosalie Siegel, Dave Allsopp, D.A. Blyler, Andrew Gallix, Richard Marshall, Jim Martin, Roy Oxlade, Kurt Palomaki, Charles Shaw, Mike von Joel, and Avery Walker, all of whom have shown unflinching dedication to the writing.

MR

Enquiries: editor@art-line.info (Ziggurat Books)

Front cover photo by Amos Chan from the film *Union City*, courtesy of The Tuxedo Company, 1979
Back cover photo by Marcus Reichert, 2003

Printed by Biddles Ltd., King's Lynn, Norfolk

Distributed by Central Books, 99 Wallis Road,
London E9 5LN
Telephone: 0845.458.9911 Fax: 0845.458.9912
E-mail: info@centralbooks.com
www.centralbooks.com

First Edition

ISBN 1 – 900439 04 – 2

CONTENTS

THE LIGHT OF THOUGHT
Introduction by Simon Lane

"Like a poet hidden in the light of thought"
                                   Percy Bysshe Shelley

In the same way in which visiting card printers suggest limits
to their clients' profession(s) for reasons of space or indolence
—"Phrenologist, Philanthropist, Phantasist"—society tends to
look askance at those who confess to a multiplicity of talent. In
earlier times, the polymath was two to a penny: a doctor was a
botanist, a parson a poet, a poet a soldier. These days, not so,
for we have evolved, or devolved, into the specialist. If it was
tolerable for James Joyce to strum his banjo (in private) then it
was always considered slightly pretentious of Paul Bowles or
Anthony Burgess to compose music as well as fiction. More's
the pity.

Marcus Reichert uses a variety of media for a single purpose: to
project himself uncompromisingly into his work, whatever
medium comes to hand. Painter, film director, photographer
and author, he achieves a synthesis within his range of activi-
ties which seems to make perfect and inexplicable sense, the
sum of his output exceeding the simple addition of its constitu-
ent parts. The means justify the ends and the sum is the sum of
human experience as much as it is of art, for Reichert has lived
sufficiently to express life in its depth as well as its breadth.
João César Monteiro, the Portuguese film director (and actor)
once described Humphrey Bogart's face as "the uncompromis-
ing manifestation of survival," which could also be a way of
looking at the totality of Reichert's work: the paintings, photographs and written descriptions of the world around him, expressed factually or in his novels, appear as facets of an imagination uninterrupted by the blink of an eye, which find form
through whatever outlet he sees fit, the various media at his
disposal squeezed like colours on a palette.

As I am fortunate enough to know Marcus Reichert and have corresponded at length with him for the last several years, I know the view he has of himself, of the world, I know it to be self-deprecating, consistent, raw, resilient, while the work itself can be disturbing, unflinching, even pessimistic at times. Yet, within it all is a taut and refined humour that never fails, even when darkness threatens to blot it out … even when the light at the end of the proverbial tunnel may turn out to be the oncoming train. It is the same humour that makes the protagonist of perhaps his most challenging and complex novel, *The Miracle of Fontana's Monkey*, an oversexed, cigarette-smoking chimp. Humour and tragedy thicken the palette.

If Reichert is brave enough to take on The Crucifixion, a timeless subject he has deftly translated through his ability to communicate mortal suffering, immortal loss—Christ's face becoming a bloodied mark of interrogation—he can also offer us paintings that are a dazzling compendium of pop, cut-up, graffiti and abstraction united by wit, dexterity and unbridled passion. Reichert's recumbent yellow nudes have a sculptural quality to them, transforming them into figures of reverential monumentality, as if they were icons carved from limestone on some impossibly distant island. His self-portraits, rhetorical and amusing, make it clear that the artist can put his tongue in his cheek; by mocking himself, he earns the right to mock others. The real intention of Reichert's art, however, is not to mock but to dissect, to examine the inside of things in order to portray their exterior.

Reichert's photography—*written light*—is the representation of a singular, visual world controlled by hidden poetry. The photographs of places invoke the Irish expression, "noted by absence." They suggest more than they offer. The simplest angle on the simplest place—the entrance hall of an old hotel, the cornice of a building outlined by a bright sky—can jolt the heart, create a terrible yearning, recall a hopeless love, a loveless hope. Of similar power are the *Portraits of Men*, not least because they tell us as much about the photographer as they do the subject. These people have lived, perhaps on the edge; they seem somehow emblematic of the human condition. The fraudulent fraction the photograph takes is the most seductive of tricks, and one of which Reichert is well aware. The real trick, however, is to take not just the photograph but also the soul. With what eternities are such moments blessed, cursed, contingent upon the dexterity of the artist.

Intentions can be variable. Only Reichert knows the story for-ever unfurling in his mind, although there is no harm in trying to guess at it. As Aldous Huxley wrote in *Meditation on El Greco*, "One of these days I may discover what the picture is about, and when that has happened I shall no longer be at liberty to impose my interpretations." The liberty at my dis-posal when contemplating the work of Marcus Reichert is one I treasure as I do all manifestations of beauty, of truth, cogni-zant, as Duchamp was, that "there is no problem because there is no solution." The light at the end of the tunnel may not be, after all, the oncoming train, but merely "the light of thought."

Rio de Janeiro
August 2005

POLITICS

DISPLACED PERSON
Introduction for a Book of Photographs

I arrived in the port of Ramsgate a displaced person. After a lengthy sojourn in the Carolinas, pitting my crucifixion paintings against fundamentalist sensibilities, I had followed a film deal to Greece. As the deal imploded, my belongings had simmered in a container on the docks of Piraeus. Now everything was stuffed into numbered crates in a warehouse in south London. Winter was descending and it was bleak. A friend owned a house overlooking the harbour but it was crammed full of artefacts he'd scavenged over the years and unfit for anyone's habitation but his own. He directed us to a vacant, rather ostentatiously furnished house on Vale Square. Here MacLeod and I would try to recover our equilibrium.

Known as the Gothic House, it was huge and draughty and adorned with a scabrous preponderance of ornamental kitsch. Opening one's eyes in the morning was like re-entering an elaborate but nonsensical dream. Weeks were spent penetrating the gloomy streets in search of home. Pedestrians spoke in tongues—the inscrutable glottal stop—and taxis were driven by duty-free smugglers fresh out of jail. The drizzle rolled off my nose and into my whisky: Ramsgate in 1997 was still pockmarked with a curious array of insalubrious pubs.

I soon realised I wasn't alone. *Home* is a kind of eternal paradox in Ramsgate, and not just because it's a port. As it had thrived during the Napoleonic War and the Great War, and survived bombardment by the Nazis, it persisted in welcoming, however weakly, the shiftless, the indigent, the certifiably deranged, many of whom in their fantastical frame of mind had come looking for a holiday spot by the sea. These souls eddied out to the very edge of the kingdom from the towns and villages from which they had escaped or been disenfranchised. Its countless imposing terraces in a state of determined dilapidation, Ramsgate was beyond picturesque. We had found ourselves on what is affectionately known as the Costa del Dole.

With frail sighs of relief, we bought the house on Royal Road and got in out of the storm. Built in 1834, it is late Regency and characteristically elegant. The grace for which that period is renowned is manifest in each satisfying architectural detail. The windows alone make each room an illuminating event, no matter how dreary the weather. From the front balcony, Spencer Square with its tennis courts and crouching shrubs stretching out below an enormous sky offering clouds of every description, one can peer down the street's gentle slope to the Channel. Hulking ferries silently glide in and out of view beyond the precipitous apron of the promenade and, on a sunny day, one can glimpse the distant cliffs of France.

Where we didn't find walls of decaying austerity, we obliterated the floral wallpaper with colour and redefined each room's geometry with an assortment of paintings too esoteric to be considered truly modern. Although *foreigners*, we were—because we did speak English—not quite so disdained as those immigrants who didn't. As we often had in other alien landscapes, we carried on from day to day as recluses, the bespectacled bald-headed artist, with his peculiar pantaloons and pretentious vocabulary, and his etiolated spectre of a wife, the impossibly beautiful writer. A few citizens were mildly friendly, but we gratefully imported our company on the wings of previous affections. With time, this was to change, and sympathetic personalities were revealed, some of whom settled in nicely amidst our oddments.

I dreamt of Nazi bombs falling below us on Paragon Street, and sirens wailing, knowing perfectly well that the sirens were only the cacophony of seagulls nesting on our roof. I dreamt of Japanese girls in shimmering kimonos walking the blossom-dappled paths of Kyoto, knowing too that they were in reality students passing below our balcony on their way to the language school round the corner. But most disorientating were my dreams of myself, shadow collapsing jaggedly from step to step, as I ranged over the smouldering ruins of the town in search of my cats, knowing all the while that they were sleeping safely on the bed beside me.

It was after such a night of dreaming that I began to photograph the unreal world I had come to regard as an unacknowledged but universal manifestation of apocalypse. I went out near dawn, before the lights of diligence had been switched on, or at night, when the glow of a television behind a rain-spattered window awakened the senses. At any moment within our house when the exquisite light glancing off the sea and down from a cloud would enter the room and momentarily possess my gaze, realisation would be transformed by the solitary engagement of my camera. Although I knew that every place is *for* this, and strangely and inexplicably *like* this, I was fascinated anew.

One day this operatic bedlam will be transformed. As always, market day will open the asylum doors but there will also be a different sort of person frequenting the stalls. The scruffy kids that linger along sidewalks filthy with their own litter, cigarettes dangling arrogantly from their anaemic lips, will be replaced by diminutive entrepreneurs sporting American ballcaps, each one intent upon a larger digital agenda. The crapped-out cars along Royal Road will vanish and silver sculptures, like soapsud-bubbles caught in mid-flight, will appear. It's already happening. In 2004, sailors no longer drown shipwrecked out on the Goodwin Sands, rather interior designers soundlessly glide in from Chelsea. Their minions begin by sweeping mouldering copies of The Sun from the rusting balconies, scouring the dried blood from the *original* tiles of the old kitchen floor. They fumigate, they proliferate, like hygienically modified drones. We will soon be living amongst the bejewelled dung beetles, yet another world apart.

5.5.04

THE ANXIETY OF SIRON FRANCO
Correspondence with Simon Lane

Subj: "Without Ice"
Date: 27/05/02 12:03:34 GMT Daylight Time
From: Simon Lane (Rio de Janeiro)
To:Marcus Reichert (London)

Marcus Matey,

What's up? Well, me, for a start. Had a fitful night, little sleep here and there; "Night is always a giant," pronounced the insomniac (Nabokov, actually). I have been feeling decidedly transparent lately (did you ever read Nabokov's *Transparent Things*?), swimming in a great big ocean of unfamiliarity, existential you might call it. I noticed, reading Borges at about four a.m., that Kirkegaard means "churchyard." So, that's it! Staring at one's own epitaph!

Speaking of death, a friend of ours got kidnapped for three hours last Wednesday. In Caracas, of all places. He'd gone up north for his son's wedding and, miraculously, had four thousand dollars in cash on him as a wedding present, which probably saved his life. The taxi that picked him up at the airport then picked up someone else with a gun. They didn't believe he was who he said he was (Siron Franco, famous Brazilian artist) so they asked him to prove it. They also told him they were going to kill him. Well, poor old Siron found himself doing a portrait of a kidnapper in the back of a Venezuelan taxi, his hand shaking like a penalty shoot out. Miraculously, they seemed to approve of the work and decided to let him go. He then took another taxi—brave step—to his hotel, where, according to the newspaper, "he ordered three double Whiskys without ice." I like that. "Without ice." I mean, was he in the mood to wait for Lightning Luis to sort the ice out? Here in Rio, there's a huge gang war going on and, worryingly, the kidnappers are coming up from São Paolo to ply their trade. As for mine—trade, that is—I ain't going nowhere without my complete published works.

Down the hatch,
Simon.

Subj: Re: "Without Ice"
Date: 28/05/02 09:50:44 GMT Daylight Time
From: Marcus Reichert (London)
To:Simon Lane (Rio de Janeiro)

Dear Simon

An interesting situation—Siron Franco with his pockets full of cash but only his gifts as a draughtsman to save him from a rusty bullet in the spleen. Perhaps, as they say of so many modern artists, he doesn't draw so good and the likeness he wrought was an object of such amusement that it brought much-needed release from the tensions robbers are subject to, although they feign indifference. On the other hand, perhaps Siron is nothing so much as a slick portraitist whose efforts only serve to flatter, which can also, I imagine, work as a palliative(?)—placating or mollifying medium. Flattery or amusement? Maybe Siron had to make several attempts at his travelling portrait of the taxi-ing robber. Maybe the taxi-ing robber said, "Siron Franco, your portrait-making doesn't cut the ice." Much worriment for the cack-handed artist, who then decides to take the more amusing route to portraitdom. Much sweaty ogling of the swarthy gunman, much scribbling, and nodding and winking and, finally—"Ha, ha, ha, this is very good, Franco. You are one funny dude!!" This may account for Siron Franco's eschewing the ice. Never again, as long as Siron Franco can remember, will ice touch his whisky.

Love
Marcus

Subj: Abstract
Date: 28/05/02 12:52:08 GMT Daylight Time
From: Simon Lane (Rio de Janeiro)
To:Marcus Reichert (London)

Dear Marcus,

Yes, this had occurred to me, for Siron is an "abstract" artist, doubtless more abstract as a result of his experience in Caracas. Various possibilities invite analysis. For example, did the kidnappers imagine that they would be in receipt of a valuable drawing should Siron convince them of his fame, something to "sell on" to a willing third party (I imagine the scene, Carlito and Hernandes nervously entering the chic Galeria Moderna Marino and proferring the sketch to some nimble secretary with the words, "What d'yer reckon? It's a Franco Siron?") Did they, indeed, have a sense of humour, which you so intelligently intimated? Were they perhaps, amateurs of the fine arts? Had they always wanted to be artists themselves, or, at least, to meet one? Were they just making fun of my poor, rich friend? I do not need to know, although of course, the next time I am in Salvador, Bahia, I will ask him, for I like Siron very much.

Four years ago, when Tunga, myself, Barrio and the late Edison Simons (psychotic, Panamanian poet, worthy of endless alliteration) did a show in Salvador, we were invited to Siron's house for dinner. Upon entering his studio, I commented in favourable terms upon one of his pieces, a collage/assemblage which was a "portrait" of Vincent. He thanked me. We dined. The next morning, the piece was delivered, carefully wrapped, to my hotel room. So why do all the nice people end up in shit street, and not the baddies? Not true, of course. What goes around, comes around, although I can't see what the hapless Siron did to deserve that little nightmare. Was he just the exception which proves the rule?

Love,
Simon.

Subj: Re: Abstract
Date: 28/05/02 15:19:15 GMT Daylight Time
From: Marcus Reichert (London)
To:Simon Lane (Rio de Janeiro)

Dear Simon

My impression is that one cannot make very good abstract art without taking drugs, preferably mescaline or psylicibin. Cheap acid, like they make in Columbia, Georgia, by grinding up empty plastic Windex (blue window-cleaner) spray-bottles then sprinkling the stuff on their Coca-Cola, only leads to more figurative doodling, like any bored person can make. You've seen it, little triangles and things with loops and swirls and ray-lines, but always, always with eyes. Siron may be a born abstract artist, which is very rare. If he is a born abstract artist then he can make a spiritual likeness of a criminal with just a few strokes, be they bold or enduringly delicate. The question I now ask myself is: would Carlito and Hernandes know themselves in the abstract, or, to put it more succinctly, in Siron's heady metaphysical rendition? I take your point that a Siron Franco abstract portrait is more valuable (chic gallery considerations aside) than a Siron Franco *aberration figuratif*, no matter how amusing. If I may, I will make a stab at answering, based on recent psychic developments and general knowledge, a few of your more pressing questions, although I am certain that, by now, you have come up with perfectly adequate answers of your own.

1. Most criminals do have a sense of humour, be it oblique or jarringly crude. Like, the difference between an aside, well-timed, and a joke recited from memory, often ill-timed.

2. Popular and commercially successful actors and singers, not criminals, are most usually amateurs of the fine arts. Criminals are already artists, often with uncanny psychological depths. When a criminal makes a work of fine art, he intends it

to mean more than its individual parts. He intends it to speak of passion, lust, caring, tears, avarice, etc. (seldom forgiveness), but as a totality, never as single items strung on the washline of sensibility—always as an integrated whole.

3. Criminals are often the shyest of fine artists. Yes, they always want to meet a so-called "real" artist. Siron Franco, as far as they knew (from what he told them, then quaveringly confirmed in pencil or ink), qualified.

4. Of course they were making fun of him, but with a secret admiration, which Siron could smell.

So how is his portrait of Vincent? Is it a spiritual evocation, or am I wrong? Maybe like the fatalistic Vincent, Siron had propelled himself into the *glimpsing void*. Perhaps Siron gave himself to his own new bride that day in the taxi, gunmen conducting the service.

Love
Marcus

Subj: O Globo
Date: 29/05/02 12:15:39 GMT Daylight Time
From: Simon Lane (Rio de Janeiro)
To:Marcus Reichert (London)

Dear Marcus,

As our gang war rages on, the Commando Vermelho having recently mounted a grenade attack on a Military Police station and the MPs, or PMs, as they are known here (we are, after all, in the Southern Hemisphere) having captured an impressive number of weapons, including rocket launchers (!) I am wondering what has happened to a smaller gang, my favourite, known as Os Amigos dos Amigos, for, however nasty these drug runners are, they are not lacking in a sense of humour. Carioca to the soles of their flip-flops. Friends of friends? Delicious conceit! Last night, PM helicopters flew below us along São Conrado Beach, lights searching for trouble, panning the hillside. Jesus! It was like Blade Runner! Even by Brazilian standards, things are hotting up, the essential threat being "crossfire," the citizens of this great city, and most of the police for that matter, keeping their heads down.

With such a background, it is indeed pertinent that we should address ourselves to the recent plight of Siron Franco. Interestingly enough, I only met the man once, which made his silent gift (his Vincent) even more touching. I aim to unearth this piece when I am in England. It is very good. Had Carlito and Hernandes had assemblage and collage material to hand, Siron could have knocked off something pretty special for them. Perhaps not such a good idea. "Work on Paper" seemed to have been more the order of the day. Yes, criminals are human, after all, which reminds me of my comment to a priest after a recent Memorial Mass, when he had talked of Jesus weeping. "Well, He was only human, wasn't he?" Now there's a conundrum.

What strikes me is that everyone wants to be an artist these days, perhaps even criminals, and, judging by what is going on down here at the moment, everyone wants to be a criminal too. Clearly, all great crimes are works of art. The destruction of the World Trade Centre is, in some manner, a masterpiece, certainly to those fanatics who perpetrated it (would this come under the "Performance" section of Art Forum, I wonder?). But I digress. Perhaps Oscar had it right when he said, "There is nothing original in art (crime), only in the means of expressing fundamental truths (lies)" but maybe I am being too arch by half.

What I must do is translate the article from *O Globo* for you, for it contains some fascinating details on Siron's sequestration. Once Carlito and Hernandes had realized that Siron was, indeed, an artist, and, deduced that he must have been a famous one, for he had plenty of cash on him and was after all, Brazilian, a man who travels and had an expensive looking case, they realized that they would have to kill him. Poor Siron! He had successfully engineered his own demise! "Now we'll have to kill you," one of them said. "Otherwise it will be all over the papers tomorrow!" Later, when they changed their minds, they said, "This is the first time we have disobeyed our commander and left someone live!" Commander? Now that would have sent shivers down Siron's shivery spine.

Elsewhere in the article, Siron says, "O nível de adrenalina no sangue era tão alto que esqueci quem eu era."—"I was so hyped up I couldn't remember who I was." Better would be "what I was." Food for thought, which I always thought a very silly expression.

Love,
Simon.

PS Nice touch: Siron couldn't remember the combination on his suitcase. Now that's playing to chance beyond the imagination, surely?

Subj: OI GABO
Date: 29/05/02 15:14:35 GMT Daylight Time
From: Marcus Reichert (London)
To:Simon Lane (Rio de Janeiro)

Dear Simon

I assume the 4,000 was in the snazzy suitcase with the combination locks, and not Siron's drawing materials. Are combination locks in themselves not the damning evidence of respectability, not to say pretension? But these are trivial matters. What really counts is Siron not remembering, first, the combinations and, second, who he was. So, you have confirmed my hunch that he was driven, without conscious forethought, to enter the *glimpsing void*. But herein, I think, lies the great paradox, because he *could* remember what he was: a maker of graven (albeit abstract) images—*et voilà*, a criminal himself, especially in terms defined by the Old Testament! "There but for the grace of God go I." Perhaps this is what subliminally, majestically, Siron communicated to his taxi-ing captors, malevolence only shimmering superficially around their yearning souls. So, when Carlito and Hernandes uttered their fatal conclusion—"Now we'll have to kill you ... " then later "... first time we disobeyed our commander and left someone live!"— they were in the throes of sublime revelation brought on by the sinner Siron, a far greater sinner, in their minds, than themselves. Not that their moment of epiphany makes Siron a less worthy soul, because, as you know by his unselfish gift of the nicely-wrapped and collaged *Vincent*, he has striven to bring a kind of simple happiness to unassuming souls like yourself—we can talk about this later, if you like—through his art.

How does one go about joining Os Amigos dos Amigos? And would such chaps enjoy rubbing shoulders with a fatalistic soul like myself posing as an artist?

Love
Marcus

Subj: Still no ice!
Date: 29/05/02 16:33:25 GMT Daylight Time
From: Simon Lane (Rio de Janeiro)
To:Marcus Reichert (London)

Dear Marcus,

We are entering dangerous territory, yeah, the catastrophe(s) of success! Siron's career, for want of a better word, brought not to a simple halt, but to a terrifying conclusion, albeit unrealized yet so unequivocally intimated and now, I am sure, unquestionably brought into question! The central dilemma becomes increasingly apparent: to whit, should he (given that he is possessed of the skills so to do) execute (no pun intended) a drawing worthy of his status as a well known, i.e. rich artist, inviting the potential, paradoxical conclusion of either

(1) Esteem in the eyes of his captors, confirmation of his being, etc., or (2) Ignorantly invite his own demise, for his captors, strangely, decided that, by kidnapping a "famous" person, they would have to do away with him in order "not to get into the papers," a pretty blind assumption if ever there was one, for, by killing him, the papers would have made more of the story, of course, not page 5 of *O Globo*, but page 1. Such an assassination would have led to our president, FHC as he is known, reaching for the red one and dialling Chaves, the Venezuelan nutter currently in charge of that odd, oily territory.

So many opposites at work, so many unresolved options! The full stop which awaits us all may become the comma, the semi-colon or the colon perhaps (I am a veteran of the exclamation mark, as those nurses, nimble spirits, sweet distributors of pain and pleasure still extant on the second floor of The London Clinic will tell you). These keyboard signals suggest hidden realities, the only reality not hidden being death, dwarfing Everest yet forever shrouded in mist. Or should I say missed.

I appreciate your suggestion of sin, for, of course, the principal sin was that Siron's captors disobeyed their Commander—capital essential in this context—and may well, themselves, be dead as I write. Such is life, such is death, when cheapened through desperation, odd legacy of childhood violently rampant! It is not life that is cheap, it is death, always (I allow myself here a contradiction). Not two sides of a coin, but two sides of two coins, of differing currency, yes, life and death, inexchangeable, wholly abstract, incompatible, useless in the purchase of things.

As for the combination lock on the suitcase, I recall with pleasure, the story my father told me at his expense—to continue the metaphor—of a case he once bought in London for the housing of whisky and gin. For a man who never bought things for himself, such an act was delightfully inconsistent with his character, for as you say, a pretentious item. He was to go, with my mother, on a holiday, in France, and thought it best to be prepared, Naturally, upon checking into some dismal lodge in Brittany, where nothing was available save for a half opened bottle of Beaujolais, a dire drink made for frustrated farters, he attempted to remember the combination. No joy. My mother considered permutations. As my father located a knife to tear at this appalling object (Swaine and Adeney, torture chamber of thirst, a cool grand or two I imagine), my mother struck upon the "key"—her own birthday. Et voilà! "Would you care for a drink, dear?" Don't imagine he hadn't included a bottle of Lanson, not exactly chilled, but drinkable, for Mum. Jesus! Back to the ice problem!

With that, a pause,
With love,
Simon.

Subj: PS & PPS
Date: 29/05/02 16:46:26 GMT Daylight Time
From: Simon Lane (Rio de Janeiro)
To:Marcus Reichert (London)

PS One does not join Os Amigos dos Amigos, one is born to be one, or born to be a friend, or enemy, of one, or others. Thankfully, we two friends, you and me, were born to be neither friends of Friends of Friends, nor enemies of the same, rather are we permitted to watch, through the thick end of the glass, their sad battling under whose crossfire the head remains bowed, the better to reach the bar.

PPS They didn't kill him, so as to avoid publicity. Yet they are dead, I am sure of it. Fine ransom, meagre exchange within the bullet-proofless glass of Siron's slumber!

Subj: Re: Still no ice!
Date: 30/05/02 07:15:14 GMT Daylight Time
From: Marcus Reichert (London)
To:Simon Lane (Rio de Janeiro)

Dear Simon

I wonder if Siron Franco will now re-evaluate his success, whether he will step off into the rocky brook of figurative art, or, perhaps, give up his art altogether and disappear into Rio's grubby suburbs to counsel the dispossessed. A "famous" person, to my understanding, is no longer in danger of mutilation or death if he gives up his celebrity and lives with the flies. Yes, death is cheap. A life for a drawing, but how many lives for how many drawings? Happiness is a warm portrait. But for whom? Always for the rich and famous, for monarchs and ballplayers. If Carlito and Hernandes are now dead, as you imagine, slain upon the Commander's orders at the sight of their exploits as depicted in *O Globo*, then portraiture is a very mixed-bag for the criminal. But it is a mixed-bag anyway. If the artist can come up with a true likeness, it most often is not flattering. If it is flattering, the work is sneered at behind the powdered hands and scented hankies. By employing collage in his portrait of Vincent, Siron Franco cleverly avoided the usual pitfalls. I have done the same, most often with the self-portrait, which is not a flattering enterprise, in my case, at best. Will Siron now see himself walking through the rancid rain of the ghetto, the cuffs of his poplin trousers in tatters, silk shirt clinging to his salty back, weary arms bearing gifts to elevate the stick and starving from their grimy mats? One never knows what the *glimpsing void* delivers up to he who finds himself, even momentarily, balanced on that precipice, as Siron Franco has.

Your father must have loved your mother very much to use her birthdate for the combination lock on his portable drinks cabinet. And she, obviously, gloried in that love, knowing that the miracle of her birth was also the miracle of his thirst. This reminds me of a marvellous photograph by Bill Brandt in which Kenneth Clark (Baron Clark) is standing by the mantel gazing lovingly down at his wife sat on the settee of their very still and very gloomy drawing-room, only the light of their love

bringing warmth to the scene. A picture brimming with con-
tentment, if you can find it.

Love
Marcus

PS I shall think no more of joining Os Amigos dos Amigos,
but only of the joys of spectating. Yes, like Cocteau and Picasso
at the bullfights!

CITIES OF THE WORLD
And the Impoverishment of Corporate Aesthetics

Although I had intended to write something ridiculous about my brief liaison with the unobliging fairies of corporate art commissions, I found myself instead caught up in the subliminal tragedy of it all. You see, fantasy is often the worst policy, and especially where the visual arts and big business are concerned. Psychological peril abounds. Big business has its very own private agenda, as opposed to its public one, and altruism is simply not the name of the game. That is not to say that corporate minds do not appreciate the viability of the visual arts as a means to charm their public and heighten their profile. The more prestigious the decoration, the greater the respect. Humour also comes into play, but it is the rare corporation that prides itself on amusing the public while amusing itself. Having a suicidal streak, I felt compelled to submit the concept with which we are here concerned to the most ominous enterprises I could think of. I am not often bound to fail, but with this enterprise I was determined to plough the abyss.

I decided to begin with the tobacco industry, now intent upon addicting the *yellow hordes*. As everyone knows, smoking is illegal in most public places in America. On April 13th, 2003 a bouncer was stabbed to death in New York City when he attempted to eject a gentlemen for smoking from the nightclub where he worked. Suffice it to say, old habits die hard. The Chinese will be *dying for a fag* long after they've found a cure for cancer. To avoid any personal awkwardness, or possible legal action, all proper names in the following excerpted e-mails have been changed.

To: Elvira Baumberg, Arts Sponsorship, Montecello Tobacco, Munich

3rd February 2003

Dear Ms. Baumberg

Max Freidkin was kind enough to encourage me to contact you. Max is a friend of Frank Lovejoy, a friend of mine, who teaches advanced English to Montecello executives. Frank loves my painting and thought the Mural Project might be right for Montecello Tobacco. One very large painting of mine was at Hotel Einstein, Berlin for many years. That painting is now in the collection of a gentleman in North Carolina whose family has produced tobacco for several generations. The imagery in the painting appears to be veiled in smoke.

The Mural Project began when I was unable to stand due to an exotic medical condition and distracted myself by "painting" on my pc. What people have found interesting about my murals is that they are not like "computer art," they are like paintings. Basically, I hate computer art. I am an expressionist, very much in the Modern tradition. The murals are intended to be very large. They are bold and full of strong colour. Germans would like them. I have done a series based on cities of the world, including two variations for Munchen. You may find the murals for Hiroshima and Dachau of particular interest. They should go down well in America too.

I hope this idea appeals to you, and look forward to speaking with you in due course.

With all best wishes

Ms. Baumberg wrote back. She said she couldn't pass my e-mail on to her superiors because of my reference to Dachau and, less distressingly, America. What was the matter with mentioning America? Hadn't America given tobacco purveyors around the world a job, for heaven's sake? It appeared I had failed in my first encounter with a corporate artichoke. Yes, I had made one deadly slip. Without knowing it, I had stupidly aligned myself with the very questionable world of *historical conscience*. Obviously, Ms. Baumberg had not appreciated what I imagined was a worthy universal objectification of the holocaust, one that might, with massive international exposure, give new meaning to such legendary establishments as Camp X-Ray. Although Chancellor Schroeder, I am certain, would see the value in such an illumination.

Had I altogether lost my mind? Tobacco, booze, gasoline, guns, all to be sold via the miracle of computer art? With whom was I to align myself to be ushered gracefully into countless high-profile eating and drinking establishments with menus sporting Neptune's Corral and Cashewed Peking Duck? If I took on the right agent, would there be a girl waiting for me in my hotel room, would I be able to specify race, hair colour, bodily proportion? As the murals were created using Macrohard Paintbox, I wrote to Macrohard—after making a couple of probing telephone calls—to ask if they might be interested in helping. In retrospect, my e-mail was perhaps not sufficiently *politique*:

To: Ms. Jacqueline Bilbo, Macrohard Inc., Macrohard Campus, Yellowstone National Computer Park

7th February 2003

Dear Jackie

As honesty is always the best policy, you should know that Linda (in public relations) and I have discussed the current problem concerning Macrohard's image in the world. I was made aware of this situation only very recently. My impression is that astute deployment of the Mural Project could go some way in endearing Macrohard anew to the public.

You will see that the murals relate to specific cities of the world. The range of major cities chosen is diverse. Naturally, the images evoke a wide range of psychological and sociological association. First and foremost however, the murals are

meant to delight and inspire the viewer. If you look closely, you will see that each mural has at least one female and one male sex organ embedded subliminally in its colourful digital fabric.

Ronnie Butterworth at Universal Graphics has informed me that the murals might be realised fairly economically using the printing technology now employed in the creation of bill-boards. This would enable us to place the murals in public spaces, like airports, with a minimum of effort—MACRO-HARD GOT YOU HERE—that sort of thing. And of course there is the element of enchantment, as the traveller marvels at the character of the place about to be experienced! Let's talk soon ...

Jackie never wrote back. Next, I decided to make a video expressing the simple grandeur of the project and chose the looming seawall in the seedy harbour town of Ramsgate on the English Channel as my location. The result was pleasing, albeit rather melodramatic, and I sent the video to my friend and fellow film-maker Angel Angelopoulos, pleasingly plump and fiftyish, who was working with a Tokyo-based media company on a *very big* digital project for the Athens Olympics. To my astonishment, Angel said he found it all very exciting. I immediately fired off another e-mail, further elaborating on the magnificence of the scheme:

'*Scale* is the key word here, as we are perfecting visual "ideas" for public places. Through the use of the computer and the placement of the image created within a site-specific photographic context, using computer technology exclusively, the impact of the work of art on the viewer is realised. One can come to terms more fully with the usefulness of this concept when imagining the problems involving the idiots working on London's Millennium Dome.'

Angel said he had grasped all that, but still hadn't hit upon a "cultural" angle to make it work, especially with regard to any collaboration between the Greeks and Japanese. Somehow we must join the two seafaring cultures of Athens and Tokyo to other unlike metropolitan sensibilities around the world, namely those of terrestrial centres like Rome. I told him my intention was first and foremost to inspire the Greeks and Japanese to co-mingle, sexually, to create a new hybrid race of vegetarians: their superficially conflicting sensibilities I saw as a great asset to this endeavour. The rest of the world would hopefully follow suit. Being a great connoisseur of such absurdity, he lauded this *concept* and I was immediately flown to Athens. Success was, against all odds, now beckoning largely.

I alighted at Ari Onassis Airport late on a Monday afternoon, the Saronic Gulf ablaze with a sweetly nullifying light. In my pocket were the keys to the house of old friends who were overseeing building works to their retreat on the isthmus below Delphi. Angel was to meet me for dinner that evening at a restaurant called L'Abreuvoir in Kolonaki. Within a radiant checkerboard of small trees strung with fairy lights and tables covered in crisp white linen we drank, ate, drank some more, and became as excited as we always had about bright ideas. Projecting our visions up into a clear pointillist night, we agreed that the cliffs of the island Salamis off Athens' port of Piraeus would be the perfect topographical beneficiary of our extravagance. The next day, when Angel returned to his air-conditioned dungeon of technology, I would venture out into the gulf on the ferry to Salamis and contemplate our precipitous site.

Before the eastward facing cliffs lies the finest stretch of beach on Salamis. The sand is fine and the sea itself without rock formations or shoals, making the water suitable for serious swimming. The road that runs along the bottom of the cliffs is accessible from both the busy harbour area farther to the west and the sparse settlement of new houses above. A parking area has been haphazardly established adjacent to a tiny shopping complex, apparently an outcropping from an ancient pavilion which, according to my guidebook, had featured a lovely colonnade and sculpted reclining figures. Angel said there had once been a lift which carried sun worshippers from the great height of the cliffs, and the bustling village a mile or so beyond, down to the glittering sea. Only a few rusty prongs of metal protruding menacingly from the rock-face remained. The setting could only be described as imposing. Occupants of the motor yachts, sailing boats, and cruise ships that engage with Athens from all over Europe would invariably wonder at our epic artwork. I happily pictured the Warsaw mural, with its melancholy fox-trot of muted colour, welcoming succulent bathers from Tel Aviv, New York, and Berlin. I telephoned Angel on my mobile. "It's perfect," I said. "I told you," he replied. And we agreed to have dinner on Salamis that evening. Angel would bring his new girlfriend Alex.

When I met Alex Zafiriou, I had an uneasy feeling. A disconcertingly beautiful twenty-three-year-old, she was, as I understood it, the product of an elderly Greek scholar and a spoiled English rose. But I had obviously got it wrong. Having grown up in America, I know an American when I meet one and Alex was undoubtedly an American. I did not pursue this reading with Angel. There was a ramshackle restaurant on the plaka above the cliffs specialising in seafood and that was where we set ourselves. No sooner did Angel have a glass of wine in one hand and a cigarette in the other than he asked me how I intended to fix the mural to the cliff.

'Hanging the mural from the cliff is actually quite simple,' I said. 'As you know, the "painting" from which the mural derives is created on a computer using, for instance, Macrohard's Paintbox. This image is transferred to diskette. The printer uses the digital information on the diskette to reproduce the mural in 60 by 40 inch sheets. This means that a mural can be any size based on that increment. Having considered the size of the main cliff at Salamis, a mural 20ft in height by 60ft in width would have the required impact without altogether dominating the site.'
'This is boring,' murmured Alex.

'Ignore her,' said Angel, which she seemed to like.

'An armature is attached to the cliff,' I continued. 'You know, holes drilled in the rock, the metal structure inserted, concrete applied—by one of your better signage contractors from Athens. The armature holds the surface on which the mural is adhered in sheets. It's the same procedure used to install a billboard. The mural can be changed whenever, but preferably four times a year.'

'To correspond with the seasons,' said Alex, and actually yawned.

So, it's more or less permanent,' Angel concluded. 'That's OK.'

'Well, it will have to be,' I cautioned him. "The Olympic Mural Project will present images by other artists long after mine are gone. My pictures will be on the site only for the first year.'

'Oh yeah,' said Angel, 'that was my idea.'

'So what are they about?' asked Alex.

'Each mural will be a work of art created by a different individual,' I explained. 'One accepts that the image may not be wholly to everyone's liking, so it's essential that each image be chosen for its aesthetic qualities, not out of political motivation. We can't have politicians commandeering the site, now can we? I can start on a cost breakdown tomorrow.'

'Why not,' said Angel.

'Yeah, but you didn't answer the question,' said Alex, addressing me. 'What are *yours* about—the first four?'

Ignoring this impertinence, I said, 'Alex, who do you work for?'

'The Southern Baptist Conference,' she replied. 'We'll be here. Are you going to contribute something meaningful?'

'Who knows?'

'There's a lot of stuff like that in London,' she went on, 'and it doesn't say a thing.'

'She's got a point,' laughed Angel. 'Basically, it's all a load of artsy-fartsy bullshit.'

'What, like the computer rubbish you're involved in?' Alex taunted him.

'Exactly, it sucks!' he again laughed, but then realised he was demeaning his gifts in her eyes. 'It's our job to go beyond the bullshit,' he added, addressing me, 'isn't it?'

'Best thing is for me to show you some print-outs,' I said. It was apparent Angel was suddenly feeling rather possessive of this person called Alex. 'But we can pursue all that later, when we've got less interesting things to do.'

'Like what?' asked Alex.

'Like take our drinks, and our cigarettes, out into the garden,' I replied. 'You can see Athens from there, from the top of the cliff. Absolutely beautiful. I discovered a path earlier, when I went to take a pee. Miniature orange trees, shadows everywhere in the moonlight—'

'Let's order a brandy first,' said Angel, lighting another cigarette.

'Fine,' Alex huffed, her eyes fixed on the hair on my chest emerging from the V of my splayed cotton collar. On the crest of her own buoyant chest, modestly exposed and shimmering in the candlelight, rested a dainty gold cross with a turquoise heart at its centre.

'You know,' said Angel 'the Muslims are the Jews of the 21st Century. What do the Muslims have that's like the Star of David? That could be our first mural: Beware Mr. Muzzie, your days are numbered.'

Alex now held my gaze.

'He's joking,' I assured her.

'It's no joke,' she snapped. 'Greeks don't see anything the matter with them.'

Angel gave me his innocent puppy dog look and shrugged.

That Friday, I returned to London to work on my presentation, but never heard from Angel again. Around the time the bouncer was stabbed in New York I learned from a mutual friend that Angel had died in his bed from an overdose of sleeping tablets. He had always said he would find true love one day.

5.5.03

BEYOND FAHRENHEIT 9/11

Aristotle: *Pity and fear are the two emotions essential to tragedy, those emotions it is essential to engender in one's audience.*

Michael Moore imposing his own practical interpretation of reality on George W. Bush should be far less disconcerting for Americans than the antagonism at work between Bush and the *real* world, that world beyond America's borders. It is not people like Michael Moore who contribute most to Bush's particular form of alienation, it is Bush's own sense of unworthiness within the context of an idealized and unreal life. Thus, as Moore's film progresses, we know, through the legitimacy of our own reasoning, it is Moore we have to side with. This inclination grows ever stronger as we come to realize that it is ourselves who are sacrificed, our lives extinguished or permanently deformed as the result of another man's moral code. We are sacrificed for an ideal. But Bush's idealism is bent, subverted by dishonesty and flushed with the excitement of deception.

Michael Moore has come to appreciate the complexity of life, having first flirted with its absurd fickleness via his own earnestly amusing theatre. Such an approach to levelling one's own neuroses is not altogether alien to George W. Bush. Although Moore must act within the confines of *real* life, Bush must not—because he has finally come to believe that he is fulfilling an important and worthy role in life. Gone are the drunken afternoons at the ballpark bar, the dirty jokes made in the midst of negotiating an oil contract, the prolonged moments of anguish when confronting the wife. Bush has come to see his actions in inevitable and irreversible theatrical terms. In fact, he has come to see himself as a great tragic hero, one most likely destined to be misunderstood. Please forget John F. Kennedy, he muses endlessly, it's my moment now.

As President of the United States, George W. Bush embodies a *mythical* form of justice. He sees his fellow world leaders as inadequate to deal with evil, the kind of evil embodied in spectres like Saddam Hussein, sworn enemy of his family and friends. Osama Bin Laden, he believes, is not only America's nemesis but his own, and that of all decent people. Bush is preoccupied with Osama Bin Laden as a man who can do no right but, conversely and paradoxically, can do no wrong. For him, it is unthinkable to acknowledge that Bin Laden, former spoiled brat, has been embraced by a vast hidden world of disdained peoples living out their lives in a perpetual state of humiliation: if it weren't for the unabated subjugation of the Palestinians, intones Bin Laden, there would have been no 9/11. As Bush sees it, he and Bin Laden are *both* mythical figures. They are gladiatorial combatants compelled by the force of circumstance—one might even say *destiny*—to fight to the death within the arena of their own twisted temple of doom. The only problem is that their arena is our world.

Theories abound on the perversity of George W. Bush's character—obviously Michael Moore has his own—but a few of us have darker theories than most. If he were not who he is, who would George W. Bush be? What if he were among America's dispossessed? What if he were a man on the edge? Many men who have suffered the consequences of a discarded life yearn for retribution—for mayhem and murder. In their minds, it is fated, the logical result of a gestation period of accumulating hatred. That person, or those people, who abused and humiliated the potential killer are manifest in the eventual victim. This, although glaringly apparent to anyone at all knowledgeable in pathological behaviour, often, in its obviousness, is beyond the realization of those responsible for meteing out justice. How does this reflect upon the psychological terrain of George W. Bush?

The act of murder is not only a means of destroying the hated, abused and humiliated self, but also, in a stroke, a means to punish the society which brought no relief. Why should fewer than half of the American people have voted for George W. Bush when he had redeemed himself, when he had, through sheer will-power and self-denial, transformed himself into a viable leader? Warfare is the punishment of an ungrateful society on the grand scale. George W. Bush is a lethal misfit, however he will never himself experience the horror and abject despair of his own society's form of retribution: capital punishment. Spoiled in equal measure to Osama Bin Laden, he will always insure that someone else suffers instead. Bush's entire life is a testament to such cowardly transference. No international court of law for himself or his people.

Bush undoubtedly sees the world in which he thrives as a malignantly superficial place—the American people, he is convinced, are not only supremely gullible, they are also sublimely culpable. He simultaneously sees himself as protector and avenging angel of the higher morality that is being desecrated and degraded all around him. For the moment, he has perhaps fastened on Michael Moore as a specimen of such moral corruption. This is George W. Bush's tragedy, his script handed to him on a silver platter: he interacts with the world in its complexity through an inverted morality, itself a reaction to the humiliation he suffered within an atmosphere of sugar-coated cynicism, and he makes an ungodly and gory mess of things. The existence of Fahrenheit 9/11 is unacceptable, but what can he do about it?

9.7.04

DROWN IN MY OWN TEARS:
Mourning the Passing of New Orléans

The idea that New Orléans might be the south's archaic equivalent to the twin towers of the World Trade Center is, at first glance, an absurd one. But absurdity often masks the most mysterious of truths. For reasons of circumstance I sadly never photographed this unbowed city of indulgence, blacks and whites lingering eternally on its outskirts in once-forbidden communion.

I photographed London's Battersea Power Station just one year after New York's shining colossi of capitalism were felled. If I'd had an appetite for apocalypse I might very well have trained my lens on Norman Foster's "gherkin", then in construction, or the stolid mass of Canary Wharf, both likely targets for suicidal devastation. But instead I was drawn to the *clichéd* hulk of the Power Station, lying with its legs held rigidly in the air like an elephant about to suddenly shift his enormous weight out of a mud hole and rise. At the time, my friend the producer Gregor Wilson was making a film in New Orléans, but my work in London kept me away. How I now regret it.

I knew the World Trade Center intimately, watched it grow out of the bowels of the subway, nearly was sucked out of its elevator's doors to my death when I was carried without warning to its skeletal 77th floor. I don't care what anyone says, it was an inhuman structure, characterless and inelegant. The huge red steel horse's head that stood decapitated on the plaza between those identical masses always struck me as Picasso's most futile work, not at all inadequate to its task, simply *futile*. Buildings anywhere near such a scale fill me with horror. Perhaps at one time the great balconied terraces of New Orléans filled another frail wandering soul with such horror, or perhaps they made him swoon with their Proustian plenitude.

It is of course the proposition of scale that awakens one through the lens to the relationship one is obliged to have with edifices of such epic proportions. The cityscape that surrounds a building that by its sheer size attains mythological status takes on a new insignificance. In the case of New Orléans, its situation, in some ways not unlike that of New York, is masked in the atmosphere of the lowlands, or so I imagine—strangely compliant, and without the need for cold-blooded provocation.

Today that atmosphere is incomprehensible to the eye: New Orléans snarls vainly, weakly at the slightest movement in a state of disemboweled mortality. Once committed, like a cat on heat, to provide the energy to keep thousands and thousands of miscreant intruders alight each year, it now lies inertly sipping its own urine. Gazing with listless eyes up beyond the fetid verge of the Mississippi and the Gulf, railroad lines curling underwater, from dawn until dusk, and then into an endless night of unendurable pain, New Orléans silently cries out for something akin to Biblical retribution. Heaven no longer waits in sultry repose in New Orléans for any man, and especially not for one George W. Bush, whose timbered ranch across the dissolute river stinks only of a few daft squirts of DKNY *eau de toilette.*

For a so-called world leader with two black people—at one time—in his cabinet, dedicated to his racist imperialist agenda, it would seem unlikely that Bush would consider the very same poor people whose children make up much of his armed forces unworthy of the most basic civic concern. However, bearing in mind his brother's nefarious (unproven) insistence that rural blacks not have the right to vote in the state of Florida, why should anyone even modestly aligned with the White House have anything to do with protecting blacks, and poor whites, from the ravages of nature—no, not when there are diffident Muslims to be subjugated, and it's far less trouble than keeping track of one's own backyard. What will young black Americans think of joining the US. Army now, and what will those poor misguided Americans who encouraged their children to dress up in flamboyant camouflage fatigues—and deploy freedom-rich digitally-adept weapons—for Uncle Sam think of encouraging their grandchildren to do the same?

One day, a sunny day, the empty fields surrounding New Orléans will be merely hypnotic, like an ancient grave-site. Imagine what this devastated land will be worth—I understand its next reincarnation is already in greedy development. The significance of such places as New Orléans in all their spiritual glory often means nothing to those lacking a taste for the exotic, the unspeakably opulent, the downright poetic. It all depends, it seems, on one's entrenched system of values but, perhaps more importantly, on where—and how far away—one sits in contemplation of the dark mysterious drift of life. For George W. Bush, in his disassociative reveries, that place must always be a bright and welcoming classroom filled with adoring children.

5.9.05

THE DEAD INHERIT THE BREEZE
On the Touring Exhibition of *The Crucifixions* to Benefit the
AIDS Services of North Carolina

Youngish black men came home to die in the town where I was
living in North Carolina. Their mothers would nurse them
right up until the end. They came in from New York, Chicago,
Minneapolis, wherever they had gone to live their lives as gay
men. Plenty of white boys were dying too, out around Raleigh
and Charlotte. For a while, there was a billboard out on Highway 64 warning of AIDS—it was directed at young people—but when the town busybodies realized they might be
advertising that they had a problem it came down. This would
have been 1993. In the summer it got so hot in that flat aimless
place that you could practically hear the bodies of dying men
melting behind the venetian blinds.

As a subject to paint, the Crucifixion had preoccupied me since
the age of eleven. It began when I was an altar boy helping to
deliver communion and was obliged to kneel for hours staring
up at a great blank wall where, I imagined, there should have
been an image of Christ's suffering to give me strength. I
should explain that my father was a painter and I began painting with oils before I could properly read or write. But it wasn't
until I was forty-two that I felt capable of taking on the Crucifixion. For me, the question was: to what extremes is one willing to go to express the agony—physical, psychological, and
spiritual. No one knows what Jesus Christ suffered. We do
know however that such a death is the ultimate expression of
man's cruelty. The anxiety and despair of being subjected to
such forms of torture and annihilation at the hands of one's
fellow human beings is *nearly* beyond comprehension. Although it is impossible to truly express such suffering, this was
my intention. I am an atheist, and have been with conviction
since I was about fourteen.

The idea to turn *The Crucifixions* touring exhibition into a
benefit for North Carolina's AIDS service organizations came

to me in the north of England. That was where I painted the pictures, with a view of desolate moorland and grazing sheep. It was in Northumberland we learned George had died. He had telephoned me a few times to ask if he should take on this job or that—Stavrinos was one of New York's finest illustrators—when all he really wanted to do was learn how to paint with oils, which he had never done. I urged him to go to our house in North Carolina, where my new studio awaited him. But it was too late. He knew it, and I knew it too.

They wanted to see my paintings in North Carolina, where I had ventured to get some relief from the dismal Northumbrian winter, but the righteous people of North Carolina hadn't any idea what they were bargaining for. It began with the ladies of the Beaufort County Arts Council, fixed at the end of the old train line in a renovated tobacco depot and adjoining station. The new "artist" in town was to put on a show for the locals, mostly golfers retired to the swamps from up north and industrious southern church people. I have to admit these ladies had balls because they readily agreed to exhibit the Crucifixions. However when it came to fully engaging in the AIDS aspect of the endeavour, the Arts Council itself stepped in and, at the top of the 11th hour, tacitly declined to be involved.

At the new Beaufort County Cultural Center, they hung all 10 of the enormous paintings in the vast space of the tobacco depot, each hovering six feet over the heads of those attending the opening, with the result that one woman ran from the exhibition, out into the warm night, convulsed with horror. The friend who revealed this unpleasantness to me stated with quiet glee that the exhibition was a great success. Over the next two weeks, consecutive articles ran in one of the local "Christian" papers—statements by and interviews with revered pastors, etc.—and the paintings were decried as blasphemous. Only the chap at the ABC Store who sold me my whisky had anything nice to say after that. Several months later, down the road at the Greenville Museum of Art, the benefit went on but the AIDS service organization itself backed out, leaving a lonely, enduringly kind married couple to represent it at the opening. The director of the Museum—Greenville being a university town—wisely satisfied all concerned by putting on the benefit but hanging only one of the Crucifixion paintings, a small study.

A lot was written in the newspapers, most of it positive, about *The Crucifixions* over the course of the tour, which traversed the entire state ending in the furniture-manufacturing capitol of Hickory. All of America has culture now, even an arid zone of anti-intellectualism like Hickory. The people who run the centers of culture are most often extremely accommodating and generous. Eventually, as the tour progressed, their halls came to be filled on opening nights with gay men. My memory lingers on the spectre of an emaciated figure poised, his cane trembling at his side, before a huge howling head of Christ. Often, these dying men would turn away from the paintings with a faint smile playing on their parched lips. I was thanked profusely by these men for making the effort, and I in turn thanked their friends who gave so unselfishly in their service. In Charlotte, where the Crucifixions were installed in their own minimalist white chapel at the Spirit Square Center for the Arts, the AIDS service organization, Metrolina, hosted an evening each year called 'Guess Who's Coming To Dinner.' At this event, ceramic plates decorated by concerned artists were auctioned to raise funds. This evening was always a great success, both elegant and inspiring. But it wasn't like this everywhere.

As the tour made its way through the kudzu-enshrouded pine forests of the North Carolina plains to the foothills of the Blue Ridge Mountains, I was occasionally asked to appear on television—the local evening news—which I gladly did. I had one story in particular I liked to impose on the interview and therefore, ruthlessly, on our audience, lolling about their living-rooms and kitchens. I told my story, making it as convoluted and, hopefully, engaging as possible. I even employed my friendliest elocution. If I'd had more time to expand, it would have gone something like this:

"You know, I live in one of the prettiest towns in the state of North Carolina. The Pamlico River opens its mouth there and just sings out to the sea. Our street is long and straight and ends on the water, after the armory—that's where East Main Street decides to become River Road. Tons of crepe myrtle blossoms, like confetti, fall on our car. A blessing, our street is a blessing.

Up on one of the crossover streets—maybe Harvey—the First Baptist Church owns some old houses, just two or three. That's part of my neighborhood, in the historical district. Those houses go back to sometime not too long after the war—the Civil War. They aren't grand, not like some of the lovelier houses in Little Washington, but they're pretty all the same. They say the church put people down on their luck in those nice old wooden houses for a while. But then, for a long time, they were just empty. I used to walk by there, glance through the windows into the empty rooms. Then, curiosity getting the better of me, I went around back and inside. Just empty houses that could have had somebody living in them. But, you know, the church didn't want that. The church wanted these houses to look like poor black folks' houses. The church wanted these houses to go down. And, you know, they did.

One day I saw the wrecking crews in there razing these diligent old houses to the ground, like dried-up useless corn. The church spent a lot of money buying these houses, just to let them fall into disrepute. And you'll never guess why upstanding church folk did this. Well, they let these pretty houses go to wrack and ruin—and finally eat the dust—just to expand their parking-lot, which was already the size of my backyard ten times over. I can't imagine what this hoodwinking of the town cost. The First Baptist Church must be very rich. Now, here's the thing: if the decent folk who worship Jesus Christ on East Main Street can spend thousands to wreck perfectly good old houses just to expand their parking-lot, how come—in the suffocating heat of August—they can't spend a couple hundred dollars on air-conditioners to keep a few lonely souls dying in abject misery from suffering any more than they have to?"

To their credit, the good people of Washington, North Carolina eventually held an auction of paintings by local artists to benefit those dying of AIDS. Black men in wheelchairs were given stately prominence at the banquet tables. When the Crucifixion paintings returned to England, they went on to Canterbury and Winchester Cathedrals, where they once more became nothing more threatening than unflinching depictions of the death of Christ.

The following poem was first published in 1993 in the catalogue *The Crucifixions and Selected Works: Touring Exhibition to Benefit AIDS Services of North Carolina* funded by Caremark Inc.

POEM IN MEMORY OF GEORGE STAVRINOS

Everyone has to die,
and some say that
we all must die alone.
Some, I think, die
more alone than others.

My father said,
shortly before he died,
'This morning, Marcus,
outside my window,
all the world was golden.'
What he saw, I knew,
was beautiful.
I wasn't to worry,
he meant to say,
he was content to die.
It was November and
growing colder.

He was 63, I was 32,
and I thought:
This is too soon,
much too soon.

It was raining,
it was raining hard and,
although it was May,
the rain was cold.
George, wry and small,
said, 'A walk in the rain—
maybe it'll do me good.'
And I thought:
All the way to 76th Street?
If you catch pneumonia,
George, you'll die.

The two sisters,
true and tall,
said goodnight to George.
Sally loved George
and he loved her.
Sister Anne could
only imagine how they
loved each other.
Sally, my wife,
and George, my friend,
for so many years.

My turn came to say
goodnight to George.
And I thought:
Goodnight and goodbye
are not the same.
I couldn't say either one.
I too kissed George,
as I always did,

and held him tightly.
We looked eye-to-eye.
Then I said,
as quietly as I could,
'Be strong.'
George said nothing,
he just looked at me.
My father had
looked at me like that.
George walked off,
into the wet cold night.
I never saw George again.

When George died
it was August,
August in New York
when the city is the hottest.
Was the world outside
George's window
golden too?
I don't know.
He might have told me,
had I been there.
Living on an island
two-thousand miles away,
we weren't meant to know.
Later, I learned
that he'd been angry,
angry near the end.
With each other,
we'd never been angry.
Maybe this was why
he never told us—
because he knew
he'd be angry.
We were both 42.
What is luck?

The boy who touched the tree
tried to make it
just as beautiful
when he drew it upon the pulp
of another tree.
'Who will understand this tree,'
he asked himself,
'this tree that is not a tree—
can it be beautiful too?'
So, father, forgive me,
no one can be content to die,
wanting for this answer.
Someone must say:
Yes, it is beautiful.

There is a secret voice that says:
Nothing you did was good enough,
but no one will remember anyway,
so it really doesn't matter.
Someone, outside ourselves,
should tell this voice to go away.
Memories are not enough
to save us, altogether, from ourselves.
Someone must help to share the anger,
help us to turn it against this voice,
help us to say: Yes, it is beautiful still.

George took a photograph
in our living-room.
The room is filled
with a golden light.
When I look at that photograph,
I am looking with George's eyes.
I am able to see with the beauty
with which George could see.
I am with George,
and I think:

This morning, Marcus,
outside your window,
all the world was golden too.

What is luck?
Is there any left?
Maybe George
took all his luck,
and gave it to me.
Maybe that was
what he was saying
when he looked
at me and said
nothing.

2003

LUCIAN FREUD
The Fearful and the Feckless

What is it exactly that I find so utterly dispiriting about the painting of Lucian Freud? What is it everyone else is seeing that I am not? What is it about this work that fills me with such emptiness, an emptiness verging on nausea? What is it about these dead figures staring back at me that leaves me lifeless, that tells me nothing of life's misfortunes, and even less of life's glories? Why is it that Lucian Freud has chosen to say nothing? Lastly, why as a fellow artist do I feel justified in writing of my dismay?

Because the magnitude of Freud's significance has left him virtually without critics, and because our social inhibitions and fears are meant to be understood and dispelled through art, not exacerbated. It was not uncommon for the unsuspecting gallery-goer to be horrified by the sudden apparition of a Francis Bacon, but it was unlikely that he, after reflecting on the execution and intent of the painting, would feel obliged to say nothing about his misgivings. But that was years ago. Today, his mouth would be fixed shut by the pressure of a subliminal elitism.

Monetary success often spells disaster for the artist, and by extension for his audience. It's a moralising cliché but money tends to have an unrelenting appetite for integrity. As John Snow said on the seven o'clock news, Kate Moss is the most famous person Lucian Freud has painted since painting the Queen. So, why paint Kate Moss, and why put the picture on the block with such alacrity? Because the process of conceiving the work and astutely releasing it into the art-buying public comprises an event, one, if engineered properly, of irrefutable significance.

Upon encountering Freud's enormous portrait of his family at Agnew's in 1985, I was shocked. I couldn't believe that a painter with his reputation would allow a picture of such mediocre technical quality to leave the studio. Areas of the canvas's surface were clotted like cottage cheese, the paint apparently applied to some other alien matter beneath. Now we know, or are meant to know, that this application was intentional. He has dignified this technique with his own face and naked figure. The surface of the picture refuses to rot, the subject achieves eternality.

The colour of Freud's endeavours sings dolorously into our miserable souls, it takes the blood out of our meagre lives to infuse the illusion he conjures with such insouciant morbidity. No, this isn't the eerie morbidity that attends a poet's fascination with death, it is the numbingly methodical perception of someone hooked on an absence of life within life, it is about the denial of sentiment. Freud's efforts may contrive an unnerving paradox for some, for others a perplexing void that excites their intellectual fibre. For me they contrive a slick meditation on Rembrandt illuminated by bad theatrical lighting.

One appreciates the tedium of Giacometti's approach because beauty, one expects, is inherent to the proposition, and this is arguably not just a matter of aesthetics, or subjectivity. With Freud, the sitter has become an essential element of the mystique. As the sitter suffers, so too the painter. However, as legend has it, the painter suffers more. Why? Because the painter isn't just sitting there, he is struggling to find something universally compelling in the sitter's physical presence. The problem with Freud is that his primary concern apparently is likeness. If the result even halfway looks like the sitter, the painter having employed his signature style, we are asked to accept that we have been vicariously granted the existence, on canvas, of raw divinity. But, to my eye, the painter has calculatingly saved the breath of life for himself, not for his subject.

But only the most tenuous connections can be made between the work of Lucian Freud and that of any other painter. He has found the secret, and that secret is entirely his own. But what good is it when it strikes such abysmal awe in so many? Certainly his secret is not about finding anything, it has already been found. It is now history. No discovery lies ahead. Can we imagine the late abandon of Picasso? Or Matisse? Will there mysteriously appear an alien world of colour and form to enrapture the painter? Will he finally disregard his strategies and succumb to the vitality of our tragic world? I doubt it. The painting of Lucian Freud, for me, exists in a vacuum, and there it shall remain. Although one might doubt the integrity of the disquietude and despair that thrives in that place, one dare not question the significance.

14.2.05

YOU ARE VERY KIND, I SAID
On the Making of Union City

Orson Welles was sitting in the corner on the top floor of Mr. Chow's, reading. It was late, well past a reasonable hour to be having lunch, or even lingering over one's coffee. I was sitting in the opposite corner, by the big window on Hyde Park, waiting for my estranged wife to arrive. The large white room, gradually turning a soft grey with the sun's retreat, was empty, the tables now freshly set for dinner.

Aren't you going to eat anything? asked Orson.

No, I'm just drinking, I replied. If you don't mind me asking, what're you reading?

Crime and Punishment, he said.

I just made a film about a crime, I said, inadequately.

Oh? he murmured, then looked at me. Why don't you sit over here?

I shrugged and joined him, wishing I weren't quite such a figure of disenchantment.

Waiting for someone?

My wife, I said. I haven't seen her for a while, a month or two.

Why don't you order something?

I'm not hungry, but I would like another drink. What're you having?

I don't remember exactly what he said, but dimly imagine it was cognac.

Sauvignon Blanc, I said to the waiter, a large one, and another for Mr. Welles.

I wanted to talk about *Union City*, but, even more, I wanted to talk about Orson and Rita Hayworth. Their marriage had ended after only two years, although they were to remain friends. Sally and I had been married for nine years, and we were just friends now too, or sort of. Orson and Rita were married in 1943, Union City is set in 1953. What was ten years in the overall scheme of things? A life-time, I now know. In 1943, Orson still had the cherubic face he had so often used to disarm the studio executives. Rita, the emerging star, had recently had her hairline raised—the most beautiful, hairiest little Spanish girl in the world. I kept picturing the enormous man sitting beside me, with his insatiable intelligence and burdening sensuality, hugging her, yearning, to his broad chest. Only a few months before, I had been standing on the rooftop terrace of Deborah Harry's apartment building in New York discussing what urgency in life is relevant and what is not, and why we are given to impulses that we know are self-destructively futile. I had wanted to make some sense to her, but I couldn't make any sense of it to myself. I confessed this to Orson.

I hope things work out, he said, when he left.

You are very kind, I said, and he was.

Union City would never have been made if it hadn't been for Deborah's willingness to take a chance on me and Monty Montgomery. And, naturally, Chris Stein was guiding Deborah along the path they would take together. We first met in the lounge of the Algonquin Hotel where Monty, my producer and friend, and I had occasionally gone for a smart gin martini, indulging in the rarefied atmosphere of Dorothy Parker and William Faulkner (who had one night in the late 1930's slept with his drunken head resting against a scorching radiator pipe in one of the bedrooms upstairs). Chris Stein had scanned the screenplay, picking out lines he found of some peculiar relevance and reading them aloud. He knew what he was looking at, and for: he is a superbly gifted *intuitif.* Needless to say, so is Deborah. When we embarked on the making of the film, Blondie was virtually unknown in the United States. *Heart Of Glass* hit number one about half-way through our shooting-schedule. From that moment on, my work became increasingly more difficult. Fortunately, the emerging star who made her way up four rickety flights every day to a cold-water flat—our primary set—was a humble soul dedicated to becoming an actress. My recollection is that the only egotist on the shoot was Mr. Cocaine.

In frame, as they say, fragility is prized, and Deborah was in gentle hands. Dennis Lipscomb, having come out of a hard touring Shakespeare company, and Everett McGill, having miraculously fallen from the heavenly gene-pool of 1950's cinema gods, were, at their young age, caring and consummate professionals. Dennis struggled compellingly within the confines of a very demanding role, and Ev brought comfort and confidence with the utterance of a single line. Both actors are now internationally known. Sam McMurray, whose leg was injured and who walked with a cane when we first met, assumed the psychology of a destitute veteran of the Korean War while subliminally communicating the nihilism of Viet Nam. He deftly conveyed war's malignant transformation of a man's sensibility, his tenderness turned to sneering disregard. But *Union City* was also about personal things, at least for me.

I had been ruminating on the nature of criminality for as long as I could remember and had come to the conclusion that it was just another ugly, albeit pathetic, everyday aspect of life—intriguing only in that it was so perversely banal. Subjugation, it seemed to me, more often than not led to violence. Sexual inadequacy too was a tricky conundrum. I recoiled at the thought that the entire world might be haunted by an atmosphere of stark humiliation. It therefore struck me as uncanny that Monty should present me with the Cornell Woolrich short story upon which I was to base the screenplay. Coincidentally, he telephoned me with news of his find at the Grand Hotel di Milano where I was visiting with my then modelling wife, next to whose room a friend of the booking agent was, in the wee hours of the morning, binding up two other blonde American *photo modelas* and subjecting them to various forms of sexual humiliation—their intermittent shrieks and prolonged fits of swearing gave the game away. Woolrich's short story was entitled *The Corpse Next Door*.

The Corpse Next Door was set in the 1930's and limited in its dramatic potential by a lack of psychological underpinning consistent with the simple hardship of The Depression era. For instance, the vagrant was merely a vagrant, not a man suffering the emotional destitution of war. I began to look around me, and found myself transported back in time. Minor horrors I had witnessed as a child revisited me. The glowing windows of apartment buildings hovering over the street on an airless New York night intimated obscenity and despair. Couples grappled in silence, locked in rooms reeking of anxiety. Their torments were bittersweet. America in the 1950's was secretly nurturing its culture of alienation. No one could have guessed what terrors it might rain down on a sunny afternoon, helicopter blades slashing an oriental sky. Communication of the healing sort was tacitly forbidden. All very cold and clinical, all deathly. This, I decided, was what the film should be about, couched in the absurdity of a sham upward mobility. Big stupid words and big pathetic emotions wrenched from the mouths of babies paddling along in the murky waters of the American dream.

I wrote the screenplay in eight days. I hadn't any money and was staying in a borrowed bed-sitter just off Fifth Avenue in the twenties. The most legendary YMCA in the world was a two minute walk away, and that's where I went to burn off all the nervous energy I somehow conjured up day and night. Monty would come by and sit on my bed on the floor and I would read what I'd written, often unable to suppress my inane giggling. But the writing was ridiculous only on one very superficial level, the underlying tone being one of disorientation and abject dread. When the picture was first shown—I can recall a rainy afternoon at the Toronto film festival—hordes of viewers left the cinema disgusted, while those who stayed eventually ceased laughing and began worrying. Many of the critics could see what we were about, but there were a few, undoubtedly ignorant of the European absurdist tradition, who found the humour, such as it was, nauseating. *Union City* went over particularly well at Cannes, and later Columbia Tristar licensed the video rights. I'd never made a feature film before, and now longed to realise the project Monty and I had originally set out to do, a life of Antonin Artaud. But that, of course, is another story altogether.

For a picture that cost so little—less than $500,000 (*Heaven's Gate* was filming grossly over-budget at the time)—and whose locations encompassed the top floor of a building comprised of railroad flats, a couple of store fronts, and a bar two blocks away, *Union City* engendered an awful lot of publicity, especially in London and New York. This, I reckon, was due to two factors. Firstly, and obviously, Deborah Harry was having her way with the world and, secondly, what we had got in the camera looked so unbelievably good. Neither did it hurt that no one could work out what the picture was about. Was it a crime picture rendered in an unnerving palette of Technicolor insults, or was it just another nonsensical art film? No one seemed to know. Now, of course, we know that it was the first *neo-noir*, a genre worthy of the coffee-table publishing format!

Much of the press coverage in New York sought to reveal how I had organised the production and with whom. The Soho News seemed to think the picture was made by a weird clique of fashion designers and their art school protégés. Nothing could have been farther from the truth. I had been in New York for barely five years, and Monty had moved to the city in 1976—we began filming in March 1979. My background was the coal regions of Pennsylvania and Monty's was the drawing-rooms and verandas of Atlanta, Georgia. We both prided ourselves on being young gentlemen, although I was by far the more unruly. Our very separate worlds began to mesh in places like the Mudd Club in Soho or, incongruously, Café des Artistes just off Central Park, restaurant to Hotel des Artistes where the high-flying poet Harry Crosby and his lover had shot themselves in 1929. We enjoyed good food and drink, and we were voyeurs.

I had a tip one night that there was a wild fairy-like creature belting out rock and roll in a club on the upper East Side and a few days later I was trying to line up a management deal for Pat Benatar. Another night, my heart hammered in my throat as I watched Tony Azito slither so very eloquently across the stage at Lincoln Centre in The *Three Penny Opera*. I later cast him as Alphonso Florescu, and Pat Benatar as his new bride. The only person no one ever asked about was the Countessa, Irina Maleeva, probably because they couldn't pronounce her name, but had they found the courage to ask they would have been told, at least by me, that she had put us in touch with the rest of our financing, and that while Fellini may have looked at her, perhaps even caressed her on the set *Satyricon*, I was obliged to actually direct her. Orson Welles had been obliged to do the same when making *The Merchant of Venice* in 1969. With Irina, you never knew what you were going to get, but it was always interesting. She was a diva without a piazza of her own, constantly on the move, like a gypsy princess. Networking was what New York was all about.

Our old friend the illustrator George Stavrinos naturally became my designer and set decorator, and brought with him everyone he needed from amongst his friends, including our make-up artist Richard Dean, who now exclusively perfects the on-screen face of Julia Roberts. Richard is the only one of George's friends who worked on *Union City* who survived the 1980's. Our co-producers are dead too. Monty got Ed Lachman's number from somebody, perhaps Kathy Bigelow, and the next thing I knew we were talking on the telephone every other day. Eddie had operated camera for D.A. Pennebaker, and most recently run second unit for Vittorio Storaro on Bertolucci's *La Luna*. Eddie liked the idea of shooting a period picture that would be expressionistic rather than purely authentic or fawningly imitative. There were extraordinary people working with us, many of them artists who would later manifest their gifts to considerable acclaim, like Kathryn Bigelow, our script supervisor, Stefan Czapsky, our gaffer, and Arne Svenson, who perfected and applied my colours and saw to it that so many essential deadlines were met. There wasn't a fashion designer among them—personal style always, never fashion!

In America in 1979, there was no protection for film directors. Now a director is entitled to his cut and if the producers are unhappy with it an audience is brought in and their response to the picture, as defined by a democratically contrived question-naire, is taken into account. This way, if the director's vision happens to be more astute than that of his producers, his work at least has the chance to fail—largely—on its own terms. Sadly, many of the most difficult scenes in *Union City* have been lost: it was decided, much to my chagrin and Monty's, that we must achieve a PG rating. Unbeknownst to us, the scenes removed from my cut were left, both in work print and negative, in the vaults of Movielab in New York. The building was later sold to Ariflex. Notice was apparently given that everything must be removed from the vaults, and that after a given date all abandoned material would go into the skip. From my research, this is what transpired. In abeyance to some desperate thirst for immortality, no doubt, the people responsible for this desecration bequeathed their share of the first *neo-noir* to the Museum of Modern Art. Both the Museum and Monty Montgomery have been extremely generous in enabling us to keep this picture alive. Deborah Harry, forbidden by contract to sing on the soundtrack, wrote and recorded *Union City Blue*, her poetical account of realising the role of Lillian Harlan and a superb gift to the film. The footage I managed to keep I have made available to Tartan Video.

2.5.05

BRETON SHOOTS SELF IN PENIS
Investigating Sex: Surrealist Discussions 1928-1932
Edited by José Pierre
Translated by Malcolm Imrie

Amusing is too mild a word to describe the disarming wit and reckless audacity of these discussions. Instantly entranced by the excited air of lightning articulacy and unguarded exuberance of the Surrealist period, one cannot help but be envious of a past that is now, within a single lifetime, nearly beyond comprehension. For some, the idea of a political art began with the perpetration of Andre Breton's drawing-room experiment. For Breton, Surrealism was a revolution. For a few contrary others, it was a charade, an ostentatious farce reeking of expensive perfume. Similarly, there is today a kind of intellectual and cultural radical who regards Breton with an informed suspicion and who, after years of coming up against his rhetoric in various mutating forms, has come to decry his pre-eminence as the principal theorist of Surrealism.

By retrieving these documents, as translated admirably by Malcolm Imrie, which only appeared in their entirety as published by Gallimard in 1990, José Pierre has done an invaluable service for those of us still inclined to pick over the detritus of the Surrealist movement, whether to perpetuate our aversion to Breton or to enlarge our understanding and appreciation of those many extraordinary individuals caught, if even momentarily, in its thrall. These discussions reveal with such immediacy the tone and texture of those minds involved as to be invaluable to anyone determined to penetrate the mystifying atmosphere of the period.

It is helpful to know that many of the discussions up until 1930 were held in the house of Marcel Duhamel at 54 rue du Chateau in Paris, which also functioned as temporary quarters, sometimes for months at a time, for Benjamin Peret, Jacques Prévert, Raymond Queneau, and Yves Tanquy. Malcolm Imrie refers to Duhamel as surrealism's "benevolent landlord", especially as he neither wrote nor painted as did most of his friends. For Breton to have initially conducted these investigations from the offices of *La Révolution Surréaliste*, such as they were, or from a public place, no matter how welcoming or stimulating, such as the Dome or Café Flore, let's say, would have been a mistake. In such circumstances, the participants would either have felt inhibited or, conversely, played even more grandly to the crowd assembled (thirteen appeared for the Second Session on 31 January 1928.) Duhamel provided a sanctuary in which this diverse group was easily inclined to intimate revelation. If there was an impediment to this shared intimacy it took the form, paradoxically, of Andre Breton. Logically for Breton, whose enquiries predominated to a dictatorial degree, only men were to share their views and experiences, contrary to the rather weak protestations of Pierre Naville and Louis Arragon, until the eighth of the twelve sessions when Paul Eluard, Yves Tanguy, and Pierre Unik all appeared with their wives. From the Eighth Session on, Breton's behavior is some-what tempered by the presence of women, but still much is revealed of his psychology and character that warrants noting.

Early on, Arragon mildly evidences his irritation with Breton's determination to define matters in his own terms and it is a telling moment:

ARRAGON: For a very long time, shame for me was a
social feeling directed against my family (the notion that
it was inferior). Later I became conscious of it when I read
books in which little boys and girls had bad feeling to
ward their parents.

BRETON: This has nothing to do with shame. It is obvious
that shame cannot be anything but sexual.

ARRAGON: Quite probably the social form of shame in me
is nothing but a disguised form of sexual shame.

BRETON: One might wish for people to have rather more self-awareness and perceive the basic form of shame underlying these so-called social forms.

ARRAGON: A wish which is entirely idealistic.

BRETON: Nevertheless, the question is far from settled. If in a discussion of shame one can claim that by definition it is impossible to overcome one's own shame, there is no way of continuing.

ARRAGON: What a shame you're so inhibited!

BRETON: What wit!

ARRAGON: What is wit?

The exchange degenerates, Arragon's ironical retorts of no purpose to Breton, with Breton finally shifting the question on shame to Peret who he insists will certainly be capable of answering.

Although his friends' good-natured responses often obscure just how annoying it must have been, Breton's attitude is often a caricature of priggishness. During the Third Session, Peret quite spontaneously asks Max Morise if he washes himself in front of the woman after making love. Breton interrupts this exchange by asking Marcel Noll if he always washes after making love, which obviously is not the same question at all. Morise, ignoring Breton, answers Peret "no". Noll, attempting to be diplomatic, feels inclined to answer Breton, and says that he does not always wash after making love. Breton then asks (one can almost hear the admonishing tone in his voice): "Why sometimes?" Either intimidated or again simply trying to be gracious, Noll answers: "Because the times when I haven't washed are when I forget. I have other preoccupations." To this, Breton shoots back: "I wonder what they might be." When Arragon comes somewhat defensively to Noll's aid, stating that he only washes when he's dirty and that a woman cannot make him dirty, Breton characteristically responds that it is only Arragon who makes himself dirty. A few moments later, Breton offers smugly that he always washes after making love, then grandly adds "except after sixty-nine." To this, Peret can't help but quip: "Of course."

Also during the Third Session a seemingly contradictory and ominously pathetic note is struck when Breton states that he doesn't cry out during sex because he knows no pleasure. When Peret, who has been pursuing the issue of embarrassment, offers Breton the opportunity to clarify this bleak statement by himself further defining the word pleasure simply as orgasm, Breton sarcastically suggests that Peret go on playing with words as long as he wants. Now blatantly contradicting himself, Breton chooses science, rather than mystifying idealism, to get himself off the hook. "Shouts, external manifestations, pretense, yes, in the sense of stimulation, of course," he intones. Consistent with the others' irrepressible good humor in the face of such arid rhetoric, when Peret asks Arragon if he is at all embarrassed by the sounds he makes, he answers, "No, because I am very proud of my pleasure. Despite myself, I sometimes say, 'Nom de Dieu!'" Such fanciful confessions—and it is often difficult to separate the true curiosities from the instantaneous flights of whimsy—are littered, disarmingly and brilliantly, throughout these wry exchanges.

Breton's naiveté, usually hidden under near-Proustian convolutions of language, is suddenly and unmistakably apparent in the Fourth Session when Pierre Naville asks the defrocked Jesuit Abbé Jean Genbach if he would submit to a woman who might approach him with the sole object of having sex. When Genbach responds that only the day before a woman came up to him, said she liked his tie, then asked to suck his cock, Breton eagerly asks if he accepted, to which Genbach answers "naturally." Apparently aghast, Breton insists that Genbach cannot call that making love. "No, I call that a small pleasure which I gave to the woman," answers Genbach. But Breton is not content with so little and pursues Genbach further, asking if such things happen often to him. Genbach answers that they do, at Plombiéres, which one assumes to be a brothel, with old Catérise. From the brief exchange between Genbach and Morise which follows, Catérise's advanced age and unloved circumstances are surmised by the reader. And although one feels ever more kindly towards Genbach, albeit while wondering at the peculiar unselfishness of his actions, Breton ruptures our contemplative mood by abruptly, in a posture of grim cynicism, taunting Genbach. "A matter of pure philanthropy, then?" insists Breton. Prévert wisely draws the conversation away from Breton and back to the unfailingly honest Genbach.

It also becomes apparent that Breton often asks a particular question, assuming his trusting friends will answer honestly and therefore mundanely, in anticipation of his own clever answer. He even goes so far as to state that certain of his questions, which are particularly absurd, are "surrealist". This in itself is a denial of Surrealism in its purest and most desirable form because it pre-emptively denies the spontaneous conjunction of disparate ideas, objects, and actions. Breton thus corrupts perception itself.

> BRETON: Valentin, what do you think of the idea of masturbating and coming in a woman's ear?

> VALENTIN (ALBERT): I wouldn't dream of it.

> BRETON: A purely surrealist question.

> ELUARD: I've already done it. It's very good ... No, not very good, it depends ...

> BRETON: It would only satisfy one side of the woman. The world is badly made.

Eleventh Session, 26 January 1931:

BRETON I have the lowest opinion of erotic literature ... To give a name to what one is talking about seems to me to be the least one can do. With some difficulty, but even with the woman I love (who doesn't like me to do so), I call a cock a cock, a cunt a cunt and so on.

This statement by Breton bears Footnote No.2, which reads: "In the manuscript, Breton has added: '(This is not true) (Second reading)', then: 'This is absolutely untrue, third reading, but I would like to.'" Breton simply lies to make good copy; one must remember that all of the sessions, once edited, were intended for publication in *La Revolution Surréaliste*. So when, during the Ninth Session, Eluard asks Breton to elaborate upon his statement that he has only been impotent once after an exhausting journey with a woman he desired but had not yet been intimate, and Breton responds that he attributed his impotence to the mauve wallpaper in the room he shared with the woman, mauve being a color he found utterly intolerable, we are most likely learning nothing about Breton, only that he is adept at poetical prevarication.

Disappointingly, Antonin Artaud, who begins the questioning in the Sixth Session, can suffer Breton's numbing magnanimity only briefly and abruptly and silently exits the session, after which the exchanges become mechanical, statistics which may be humorous at moments but revealing of very little:

BRETON: You have not made love for some time. How many times can you do it in one night (from nine in the evening to nine in the morning) and on each of the three following days (from nine in the morning on 3 March to nine in the morning on 6 March)? Can you make love every day? Without any exception? How many times per day? What is the maximum you've managed in twelve hours?

PREVERT: I don't know how many times I can make love. Between nine in the evening and nine in the morning means nothing to me. I usually make love once or twice. I hate sport.

PERET: In general, three or four times. More or less the same during the next three days. I don't think I could make love every day for a year. Nine times in five hours ...

Artaud's concerns, unlike Breton's, do not engender frivolous responses, neither does he entertain romantic posturings which are meant to self-engrandize, and his arguments are anything but laconic. In fact, it is difficult for Breton to get a grip on what he is saying:

BRETON: I have never so to speak experienced sexual "pleasure". I may not have been certain of loving every woman with whom I've made love, but I've been far less certain of not loving her.

ARTAUD: In speaking of sexual pleasure, Breton, are you only thinking of the physical aspect, or do you never think of the physical aspect, or is it that in the sexual act the mental pleasure you experience encompasses everything?

BRETON: I cannot conceive of any pleasure except normal pleasure.

ARTAUD: That answer seems to me extraordinarily tendentious and arbitrary.

Earlier on, of course, Breton talks about how perversion in the sexual act is most desirable and elevating. Obviously, face-to-face with a man of Artaud's singular perceptions, Breton wishes to appear the mediating force of decency.

It is too easy, however, to criticize and condemn Breton in the context of Artaud, a context without applicable boundaries and restraints. Artaud's concern with sex is synonymous with his concern for the disintegration of the human spirit (Artaud was

a philosopher and innovator of an arguably theosophical bent),
while Breton's concern is with a fictionalization of humanity's
sociological preoccupation with sex. Breton is about the unprecedented conjuring of a deluge of ridiculous and obscene
couplings over which his pedestal might rise, the beacon of a
modern divinity beaming overall. Breton is not merely a socially astute artist determined not to have technology up-
stage him, he is an artist who, lacking any sensual preoccupation, has determined to use society as his medium. Bearing
this in mind, these twelve sessions make convincingly apparent
the transparency of Breton's motives. That this egocentricity
should have been overlooked to such a large extent by his
friends and colleagues throughout these sessions is a testament
to their own inspired willingness to unselfishly reveal themselves in the cause of a poetry yet to be written and painted.

During the Eighth Session, with the contributions of Nusch
Eluard, Jeanette Tanguy, Madame Unik, and Simone Vion,
these accountings become livelier and far more amusing.

Question 6. How many times have you been able to come con-
secutively, without leaving the room?

> TANGUY: Six times (between ten in the evening and
> eleven in the morning, when I was twenty-two) ...

> Mme TANGUY: Four times (between nine and eleven
> years old, between nine o'clock and eleven o'clock).

> ELUARD: I'm ashamed. Eleven times ...

Early on in this session, having asked the nine others present
what explicit sexual image they find most stimulating, Breton
is so intent upon establishing the supremacy of his own per-
sonality that he feels compelled to correct those most stimu-
lated by the eyes of the imagined lover. The eyes, he baldly
states, are not sexual. Here he not only contradicts himself
(in the Second Session he stated that he was most excited

by the eyes and the breasts), but betrays his idealization of sex as an activity necessarily and essentially bound up in love. In the earlier session, seeking to obscure his innately bourgeois prejudices concerning the act of sex itself, he quickly added that in addition to the eyes and the breasts he found "everything in physical love which pertains to perversity" exciting. Similarly contradicting himself during the Eighth Session, Breton states that he is very much in favor of mutual exhibitionism, although he rarely practices it, but more importantly makes it clear that with a woman he loves the idea of seeing her sex and showing her his own is "truly scandalous". Such prudishness drenched in sticky romanticism is one of Breton's most consistent qualities. He is both excited and repulsed by that which he finds dirty about the sexual act and, particularly, about women.

With regard to women, during the Seventh Session, in the midst of a discussion on cleanliness and desiccated fecal matter, Breton wanly interposes the thought that perhaps it shouldn't be impossible to love a woman who is dirty and who stays dirty, as long as she isn't stupid. He wishes to love a woman enough not to care whether she is clean or dirty. He feels such aversions are childish, in others, and can't "see any difference between the encrusted shit of the woman one loves and her eyes". However, later on in the session, in response to Georges Sadoul's remark that he finds a depilated or shaved sex completely disgusting, Breton gasps: "It's a scandal that there are still unshaven sexes!"

Obviously, when the truth comes rushing from his mouth, Breton's sophisticated fantasies can't quite accommodate the physical realities. This is perhaps why he feels that brevity is preferable, stating during the Sixth Session that although foreplay might take a lot longer than half an hour for him, the act itself takes a maximum of twenty seconds. When asked about the second time, if there were one, Breton, firstly qualifying his response by proposing that one accepts that one makes love in the shortest possible time, confesses that it might take three to five minutes. This is of course if he doesn't fake it, as he states he is quite capable of doing in the Seventh Session. And if the woman isn't a negress. But, as he stated in the Fourth Session, he wouldn't be having sex with an African anyway, not under any circumstances—a non-white woman maybe, but not a negress. Bearing in mind that Nancy Cunard fell in love with Henry Crowder in 1929, and she wasn't the first socially prominent white person in Paris to flaunt her affections for a black, Breton doesn't come off as much of a sexual revolutionary.

Most laughable in light of Breton's various unformed views and adolescent confusions is his terse answer to a question put by Gui Rosey in the Twelfth Session, especially in the context of the others' answers:

> ROSEY: Is a woman's orgasm more intense than a man's? Breton?
>
> BRETON: Less intense.
>
> ELUARD: Don't know.
>
> TANGUY: Less violent, but longer.
>
> ROSEY: Much more violent and longer.

One begins to worry for and wonder about the future Mrs. Breton. What is most deeply perplexing however, when truth is meant to be the sole drink of the evening, is Breton's uncanny ability to transform a cherished sexual perversion in one instance into a loathed degenerate practice in another:

First Session, 27 January 1928:

> PREVERT: What do you think about mutual masturbation and fellation between two men? ... Would they be homo-sexuals?

BRETON: Yes. For me, homosexuality is linked to the idea of sodomy.

Second Session, 31 January 1928:

BOIFFARD (JACQUES-A.): ... I absolutely do not condemn homosexuality from a moral point of view. I too have imagined going to bed with a man without any revulsion. Though I haven't done it.

BRETON: I am absolutely opposed to continuing the discussion of this subject. If this promotion of homosexuality carries on, I will leave this meeting forthwith.

Ninth Session, 24 November 1930:

VALENTIN: ... How favorably do (you look upon homosexuality) and how do (you) imagine such relations? ...

BRETON: ... For men: unrestrained sodomy. I find the whole thing utterly repugnant—active or passive, they're all fucked.

Twelfth Session, 1 August 1932:

TANGUY: Sodomy isn't homosexual. It's because it's a woman that it appeals to me ...

BRETON: ... I prefer sodomy first and foremost for moral reasons, principally non-conformism.

Then there is the more contemporary consideration of Breton's insecurity, both with women and with himself. In this regard, there are a few moments worth examining, moments I found particularly compelling among Breton's more revealing ones. When Peret allows that he always follows the woman's preference in love-making, that he in fact often asks her what she prefers, Breton finds it unthinkable that a man should do such a thing—he feels that it would only unnecessarily complicate matters. Unik asks why he finds this so extraordinary, and Breton answers, as if to dismiss the issue, that it is wholly inappropriate. But when Unik insists that the opposite might be true, Breton bristles and shouts "I don't give a damn!" Likewise, Breton has a very real problem with the woman taking the initiative. Breton asks Morise if he allows a woman to touch his penis when it is not erect. Morise, without hesitation, responds "Why not?" Breton then asks the same question of Peret, who confesses that he would feel "diminished" were this to happen. "That's exactly the right word," says Breton: *diminished*. Arragon's response, as is often the case, is the most winning: "If a woman touched my sex only when it was erect, it wouldn't get that way very often." It seems that Breton hated to be caressed at all.

During the Eighth Session, in response to Eluard's asking what sort of caress his friends prefer, both men and women, Breton curiously states that he feels that sodomy has the "greatest possibilities, although I don't like it", then pompously rejects the word "caress" and Eluard's question, stating that he doesn't like anyone to caress him. "I hate that," he says, seemingly without reservation or embarrassment. Later in the same session, Breton grandly offers that if he desires a woman it makes no difference to him whether she comes or not. Both Andre Thirion and Eluard voice their misgivings about such an attitude, Eluard attributing such apathy to a profound pessimism. Breton responds by ridiculing a story by Boccaccio about a young man who falls asleep while still inside his lover. If such a "really crazy" thing were to happen to him, says Breton, he would kill himself upon awakening. Experience tells us that unless his member were as long as the Amazon and his lover the very Spirit of Drought, such a moment would surely elude him.

Andre Breton, Surrealism's best organized and most vociferous exponent, was first and foremost a politician. Organized art movements are necessarily political. And, although Breton was by no means a political theorist, or at least not profoundly so, he was an uncannily astute opportunist who in his transience easily passed for a philosophical force. Once one is able to strip away the linguistic encumbrances of his writing and come directly to terms with the synthetic skeleton upon which they are hung, one finds the most prosaic of "surrealist" thinking. Breton's critical capacities were honed to separate himself and his allies—or troops— from those individuals condemned by circumstance to struggle in isolation with their own particular art and vision—in a phrase, those most likely to fail in the social arena. When Bejamin Péret's mother sent him to Breton hoping the celebrated young poet would help her son to find his way, Breton quickly made Péret his Adjutant General, and by all accounts Péret was a brilliant one. Unlike the garrulous Appollinaire, whose writing was innately radical and instinctually revolutionary, and Gide, whose elegance was intrinsically subservient to his dignity, Breton sought esteem through subtle imitation. By elevating, as if borne upon his own scintillating intellect, the obscure genius of outcasts and recluses like Gérard de Nerval and Isidore Ducasse, Breton was able to divert his public from the orthodoxy of his own sensibility. Perhaps most admirable was Breton's early quest for realization of an idealized love, his idea, borrowed from the universal given, that love alone is capable of reconciling a man to his life.

In conclusion, there were two exchanges during the sessions that were particularly telling, and they need no comment:

BRETON: Must love necessarily be reciprocal?

NAVILLE: I do not believe it is absolutely necessary ...

UNIK: There is absolutely no need for love to be reciprocal.

PERET: It does not have to be reciprocal.

BRETON: It is necessarily reciprocal.

BRETON: I would like to ask Queneau what logic he in
tends to substitute for bourgeois logic.

QUENEAU: None at all.

BRETON: So how would you reply without logic to such
questions?

QUENEAU: Through a degree of trust in people I consider
my friends, without any sentimentality.

BRETON: That is impossible.

Investigating Sex: Surrealist Discussions 1928-1932 is published by Verso, 6 Meard Street, London W1V 3HR and 29
West 35th Street, New York NY 10001-2291

1994

GENERAL RULES OF THE SCHOOL OF ABJECT EXPRESSIONISM
Towards a New Parochial Art

The School of Abject Expressionism lives and works by its own very particular rules. It exists to breathe life into radicality without apparent artifice or motive. Woe be unto him who mixes politics with painting, for he shall surely flunk life's final exam. Obviously, we do not draw or paint from nature. On any given day, the garden is green, the sea is green, beans in a bowl are green. We know this without reference to source. Occasionally, we might be struck by the significance of some object and render it accordingly. Impossible objects, like light-bulbs when illuminated, are good. Anything electrical is worth pursuing, be it dangerously utilitarian or benignly prettifying, like a shaver or hair-dryer. No shape is without dignity, neither is any colour. Ask Picasso. Defining anything with black is good. As Pablo said: When in doubt, use black. We detest Cezanne's mountains. Modern Art should never be considered as such because it generates a kind of false optimism in the world. Outsider Art is best, especially if it addresses the awkward subjects of religion and sex. Pictures produced by the criminally insane are especially interesting. It is a little known fact that Ronnie Kray painted at least one masterpiece, a work simultaneously reminiscent of Van Gogh and Soutine. Blood is too seldom applied to canvas. The legendary conservationist Peter Beard revolutionised photography by applying his own blood to his photographs: on goes the blood and, hey presto, it is no longer just another self-regarding snapshot but a work of overt narcissism. We do not use technological wizardry to apply our paint, however the introduction of extraneous visual matter—newspaper clippings, x-rays, pages from girlie magazines—is perfectly acceptable; however the introduction of such matter must necessarily have a morbid or perverse aspect. Never draw or paint the entire human figure unless expressing vulnerability or inaccessibility: how many of us make love to an entire person? Avoid anything shiny: sparkles, aluminium foil, etc. are strictly forbidden. Avoid having anyone watch you

when painting: no one knows how the greatest paintings in the
world were made and it should remain so. Beware of animation
of any kind: we are not cartoonists. Yes, when in doubt do
paint or draw but remember: if there isn't something peculiar
about the result, there isn't something interesting about yourself. The ultimate goal of the School of Abject Expressionism
is to bring happiness into the hospital.

11.4.04

CONVERSATION FROM THE MARGINS:
D.A. Blyler interviews Marcus Reichert

In many ways, talking with Marcus Reichert about his art runs contrary to the work. When so much Art is spun by media-savvy celebs, Reichert's oeuvre emerges from the chest. An emotional response is inevitable. And the emotion isn't the result of a cunning strategy to manipulate or shock, but rather to illuminate his subjects and the feelings they evoke within him. This having been achieved, it is hard not to share with Reichert his interpretation of the world—the visual world, but also the world of the mind, and the spirit. *D.A. Blyler*

DAB: Man Ray once commented that he painted what he could not photograph, "that which comes from the imagination or from dreams, or from an unconscious drive." And that he photographed the things that he didn't wish to paint, the things which already were in existence. Do you separate your painting and photography in similar fashion?

MR: Absolutely. Painting for me is very like writing. Psychologically, there is a texture to painting that must be an immediate manifestation of the subconscious. Like a poem, a painting has a particular confine. The world has none, and this, for me, is what is most exciting about taking pictures. The photograph creates the confine, stolen from reality.

DAB: The aspect of your photographic work that I find most refreshing is its lack of any overtly moralistic, political, or sociological stance. So often in today's art we find such posturing almost obligatory. In a sense this posturing appears to be a reaction to what many people might refer to as the "egocentricity" of art, but you make no bones about the fact that the subject matter of your photographs is entirely egocentric. Do you believe artists have a moral imperative to create socially relevant work?

MR: Yes, perhaps we do have such an obligation, but fulfilling that obligation can take myriad unanticipated, and, occasionally, unprecedented forms. I am very uncomfortable with art that hovers anywhere near propaganda. Take Picasso's Guernica, this is a work profoundly sensitive to the suffering wrought by Franco and his Nazi cohorts, however there is nothing explicitly political about the painting itself. It is a work, in the suffering depicted, of great spirituality. This is its real power. Poussin's The Rape of the Sabine Women, Gericault's The Raft of the Medusa, and Matthew Brady's photographs of America's Civil War dead also come to mind. All of these works address cataclysmic human suffering with admirable formality and invention. Picasso's genius was to bring cubism into this arena of social consciousness and personal empathy. But these are pictures that deal with tragedy, they are not pictures that express a kind of social bitterness. Although I would welcome the chance to take photographs in the midst of such pathos, I have so far restricted myself to the pathos intrinsic to what I see as beauty. Taking a particular kind of photograph now means risking one's life, or worse.

DAB: Would you say then that you agree or disagree with Henry Miller's "Open Letter to the Surrealists" where he wrote that the artist is the opposite of the politically minded individual, the opposite of the reformer, the opposite of the idealist? The artist does not tinker with the universe, Miller claimed, but recreates it out of his own experience and understanding of life.

MR: A typically bombastic statement. No, I don't agree with Miller. When he wrote that, the Surrealists, as a whole, were possessed by communist fervour. This would carry on with the Existentialists, Sartre in particular, for decades to come. I think it was Breton's politicisation of the arts that Miller objected to primarily. Artaud was even more vehement in his denunciation of Breton's naive love affair with communism. Most artists struggle with their conscience and this struggle necessarily embraces idealism in one form or another. The Marquis de Sade was an idealist. One can be politically minded, can support reform, and not be involved in the public dialogue. Certainly the artist does tinker with the universe because he occasionally transforms our perception of ourselves in relationship to the world. This can be accomplished in very subtle ways.

DAB: I'd like to talk a little a bit about your formative years as an artist. Though you graduated from the prestigious Rhode Island School of Design it was on an independent study track. To a large degree, we could say that you have had no formal, "institutional" training as a painter, not to mention as a filmmaker, writer, or photographer. Was this a conscious decision? And how do you assess the impact of those politically sensitive cottage industries, otherwise known as "Creative Arts Programs," on the contemporary Arts scene?

MR: I have no way of assessing the impact of "Creative Arts Programs" on contemporary art because I've had so little to do with such things. Whenever I've attempted to give something of value to the public, the bureaucrats meant to be aiding and abetting the process have been standing sullenly or gleefully, depending upon the perversity of their dispositions, in the way. No matter what lengths one goes to, from my experience, nothing ever happens. The tour of paintings to benefit the AIDS services of North Carolina was funded by a company that made billions manufacturing and distributing morphine-injecting machines for the terminally ill. As for education, I went to the Rhode Island School of Design rather than Viet Nam. Not much of a choice. In the end, the U.S. government made every effort to put me in a uniform anyway. I had absolutely no interest in art school. I already knew how to paint, thanks to being the son of a painter and sculptor. Not that I knew how to paint properly. My father just left his paints lying around. Without painting and writing, I would very likely have ended up in prison. I once was deeply anti-social, I stole, and I nurtured my intellectual appetites on highbrow pornography. For me, taking photographs was like finding God.

DAB: It's interesting that you should say that highbrow pornography whetted your early intellectual appetite. Diane Arbus said that she always thought of photography as a "naughty" thing to do, and that early on she took a perverse pleasure in clicking the shutter. Yet, we don't see Arbus's voyeuristic tendency in your photographs. Instead, as Mel Gooding points out, your photographs possess an uncanny quality, as though you were not there to take them. How would you describe the relationship of the photographer to his subject matter? Obviously it is different than that of a painter's.

MR: I readily admit to being hugely voyeuristic. I spend hours just sitting and watching. For me, the problem with Arbus's photographs is that they aren't sufficiently subtle in their voyeurism. Her pictures are blatantly sensational and—here's the "questionable" bit—exploitative. I, personally, don't have any problem with that, because people readily participate in such set-up situations. But many of her pictures actually aren't very involving. I think what Mel Gooding is getting at is the uncanny ability some photographs have to bring us into the moment, and the more quietly we make that entrance the better. It is always easier to stare at something when one remains unnoticed, and when intimate with the subject, there is no intrusion. Nan Goldin has a knack for getting herself inside an intimate situation. William Eggleston reveals intimacy of place in such a way that we simply and gracefully walk into it. As a painter, my subject matter is not physically referential, it is psychologically referential. My photographs address a kind of pure formality that my paintings naturally do not.

DAB: Can you expand some on what your paintings do address? You say that your paintings are "psychologically referential" but who, or what, serves as the ultimate reference point for this psychological rendering? Would you say that you, the artist, are the subject of your work? Or does the painting itself (as Jackson Pollock argued) take on a life of its own—therefore becoming its own ultimate reference point?

MR: My paintings address my own peculiar needs as a painter. On one hand, painting is a sensual pursuit, on the other, it is an avowedly intimate revealing of one's self. What I mean is that making a painting—the kind I make—is a kind of stripping away of the thick skin we develop to survive in a world increasingly uninterested in dignified personal revelation—poetry, if you will. That stripping away, in psychological terms, can be just as violent as the world is violent. It occurs to me that this is an equation of sorts. So when you ask how exactly my painting is "psychologically referential" the answer must be, as Jackson Pollock says, that the painting is a living manifestation of not only what I might reveal but also what the viewer brings to it.

DAB: How much of this rendering is a conscious decision on your part? I'm particularly curious as to how you view this in the context of your Crucifixion series.

MR: I was not conscious of myself when I painted the Crucifixion. I was conscious of my body, because the destruction of a man's sinew is something that must be felt if it is to be drawn, but I was not aware of much else, other than the suffering I needed to see in Christ's face. The formal aspects of the painting were altogether subservient to the expression of suffering.

DAB: Be it the Crucifixion series or any of your other paintings, would you say then that the work is begun with its outcome unresolved? You have no preconceived psychological impression you wish to reveal through your iconography, as Salvador Dali, it seems, did?

MR: Unlike the painting of Dali, mine is not narrative. I save that sort of struggle for my writing. But even when I'm writing fiction, I rarely know in advance where the work will take me. I tend to paint in series because it gives me a liberating format in which to experiment. If the canvases are all the same size, that helps. Over the last few years I've been making both figurative and written notes on the canvas long before the actual painting begins. I might go into the studio after a late night and just start in drawing on the blank canvases with whatever is to hand. Several weeks, or even months later I might move on to the next stage. If I sense the picture is becoming about something, I try to understand what that might be—often by carrying on painting,. Suddenly an image might strike me as rather melancholy, or menacing, or, in its diversity of signals, perplexing—it's then that I begin to appreciate the psychology at work in that particular painting, not before. For me, it's essential that the evolution of the image is a mystery, an unfolding mystery, even if the image is something as simple as an empty vase on a table.

DAB: One aspect of your paintings that has always drawn me to them is their ability to rouse an immediate emotional response, and afterwards to evoke a philosophical reflection that's akin to the "unfolding mystery" you mention. I'm curious which artists have impacted you, be it in your youth or maturity, and what particular quality in their work drew your attention.

MR: Vincent Van Gogh was important to me from very early on. Coincidentally, he taught for a time down the street from our house in Ramsgate. I never once passed No.6 without thinking of him. His determination to paint with what I would call a poetic assault on the senses was extraordinary. And his isolation along this road to revelation was something I related to, utterly and completely. Even now, when I come upon one of his pictures that I find particularly poignant I want to begin painting all over again. The same unrelieved atmosphere of sacrifice informs the drawing of Antonin Artaud. When he drew someone, or himself, he found a true landscape of the soul. Artaud wrote about Van Gogh in 1947—*The Man Suicided by Society*—and this helped bring about a re-evaluation of his work. Kindred spirits. Jack Bilbo is a painter known to a passionate few who collect his work and treasure his various publications, like the rather grand autobiography he produced, now often seen on the library shelves of aficionados of *outsider art* and *arte brute*. Bilbo takes the fear out of one's appetite for poetry, for images that are singularly personal and, conceivably, irrelevant. Jean Dubuffet's early work I find altogether engaging in its possession of the absurd. He painted like a child with the sophistication of a saint. His later pictures, the big commercial gallery stuff—the *designed* paintings—leave me cold. I'm fortunate to have Roy Oxlade and Rose Wylie as friends, both of whom paint with the kind of wilful disregard for convention that I admire. All of these artists are concerned with seeing, with getting at the essence of the subject. They all had to find their own way, even if that way appeared altogether alien, even if it brought them nothing but trouble. Naturally, I could go on—Chaim Soutine, early Pollock, early Bacon, Von Gebhardt, Giotto, Picasso's Dora Maar pictures, some Matisse, etc.

DAB: Returning to the subject of photography. Neil Postman talks about the art in his seminal work *Amusing Ourselves to Death*. In it he writes: "Language makes sense only when it is presented as a sequence of propositions. Meaning is distorted when a word or sentence is, as we say, taken out of context; when a reader or listener is deprived of what was said before, and after. But there is no such thing as a photograph taken out of context, for a photograph does not require one. In fact, the point of photography is to isolate images from context, so as to make them visible in a different way." Postman's words seem to have particular relevance within the context of your work, where we see so many images (a chair, a fence, an empty room, a woman's calves) that upon the surface appear banal yet also imply layers of meanings. As a novelist and screenwriter, do you find that your photography can plumb depths unreachable to the written word?

MR: I agree completely with Neil Postman. A photograph has a kind of purity that is at a remove from writing. Not, perhaps, alien to writing, but without particular encumbrances. The question of how a work of art actually functions must necessarily come into it. This then brings us to the subjective/

objective dilemma. Writing and film-making are both highly subjective pursuits. The world's objective interpretation of the work is a proposition fraught with misinterpretation, with misreading. Any artist in his right mind accepts this. What is in a look? Is a look ripe with simple affection, or some hidden need, or unabandoned lust? How is one to know? Hopefully, coming upon a photograph that one finds particularly exquisite is like coming upon the moment itself. The photograph, if it works, excludes everything but the beauty of that moment. So, yes, the photograph can accomplish something exclusive to itself, something unencumbered in its singularity.

DAB: In Toni Morrison's novel *Tar Baby*, she writes that at some point in life the world's beauty becomes enough; that you don't need to photograph, paint or even remember it. It is enough. I wonder if an artist such as yourself, who has involved himself in so many disciplines, is strangely enough striving to reach such a state, whereupon the desire to create art has become mute?

MR: I have always felt that memory is a con. That is, the idea of memory as a reliable force informing one's psychology is such a frail thing at best that it can be the source of untold frustration: memory, paradoxically, is really of no comfort We can't remain within the confine of memory for very long and so, as ever, we are left longing for what is gone. Obviously, what is present exists without memory. A photograph exists without memory, so does a painting. These things, like the moment, confound our mortality. How can we be bored, how can we possibly feel agitation and ennui when we're surrounded by such beauty, even the agonising beauty of the horrific? Maybe we go on making art because we find the world in its beauty somehow overwhelming: we capture beauty and possess it in the moment of our own absurd creation. I think the moment to which Toni Morrison refers comes either very close to the end or, for a few, when time, in its abstraction, has ceased to exist. In that moment when I take a photograph time ceases to exist. But really there is no need for the camera, because seeing is enough. The camera gives me something to do. The most terrible thing would be to live with blindness. I sometimes close my eyes and childishly experience what it would be to live only through sound and touch. Memory takes on a whole new dimension.

DAB: You have spent much of your working life as an artist abroad. And many of the photographs in your last book (*Reichert: The Human Edifice*) are from foreign locales: Paris, Athens, Madrid. Even your photographs of human figures suggest a strong sense of place. In large part, it is from where your work draws its power. As William Kennedy keenly notes, without a sense of place art is often reduced to a cry of voices in empty rooms, "a literature of the self, at its best poetic music; at its worst a thin gruel of the ego." In what ways has your life as an expatriate, away from familiar soil, distilled this sense?

MR: Nearly every place I go feels somehow strangely familiar. I think for many photographers it is the strangeness in the familiar that excites the picture-taking instinct. Although I am excited by those moments of domestic revelation, I tend to find greater poetry in the sensation of being disembodied, and this occurs most often when I'm in a new city. Catching sight of someone with whom I'm intimate in an alien setting is also terribly compelling. That person often assumes a new solidity, edges as it were. So I do very much appreciate what William Kennedy is saying. I believe place lives in the imagination— I've written innumerable detailed scenes involving real places I've never been—and for me there is almost always an eerie sense of *déja vu* when a particularly powerful environment presents itself to the camera.

DAB: Susan Sontag has written quite expansively on the art of photography, but the one observation she's made that has struck me as particularly telling is that although for Mallarmé everything in the world existed in order to end in a book, today everything exists to end in a photograph. I've always found it a wholeheartedly depressing commentary on modernity. Do you view your photography as a logical extension of your work as a poet, or something altogether different?

MR: I see everything I do as one thing: my perception of the world as manifest in metaphor, be that metaphor literary or pictorial. As a poet, one deals in paradox. We perceive a con-fabulation of meaning in things that very likely doesn't exist, or that exists only for us. And all of it is tinged with emotion, which naturally informs our philosophy as artists and poets. Often, what we create is unlike what we perceive. We find a new world of meaning in the creation. The word poem literally translated from the Greek means dried blood. It is the residue of what we perceive, of what we feel. The exaltation of birth, the humiliation of slaughter, it all finally exists as a kind of residue. Memory is this residue. The photograph is this residue as well. A good photograph therefore is a good poem.

Chachoengsao, Thailand / London, England
November 2003

Tambon Nam Muang, Thailand / Marseille, France
August 2005

PORNOGRAPHY

From VERDON ANGSTER
Chapter Nine, Belmar Road

The fire for which all thirst; now beams on me,
 Consuming the last clouds of cold mortality.
– *Adonais*, Percy Bysshe Shelley

At once there was darkness. Fear took hold of me. The darkness turned glassy and hard. Some part of me said, step right through. But I knew I couldn't; I was afraid. What had once been a hand disappeared behind me in a strand of brilliant light. The same part of me said, forget your hands. My fingertips were already miles away. Warmth emanated from the darkness, warmth as possessive as the warmth of the womb. I feared it too; at least the cold of the river was familiar. My hands returned to fight the glassy darkness that was swimming with my sweat. The doors gave way, the double doors of Virginnia's room with their frosted images, herons etched poised as if waiting for the glass to turn to water. A wind was at my back, driving me down the steps, into darkness. At the bottom lay the bower of japonica where Virginnia had transformed herself into the geisha. The Iris Room was the Riverhine, consumed by black fire. When I struck at the panels of the screen, with their translucent tendrils, they turned to mud. The tendrils reached out to claim me and the silt sucked me down into its warmth.

The rusted hulk of a pivotable railroad bridge lay flat against a backdrop of ice and brown stone. It took me a while to understand what I was seeing. Then I realized I hadn't drowned. Only when I'd mustered the strength to turn my head the other way did I see that the boat Lydie Fay and the Fox and I had taken to the trestle was drifting just yards from me along the shore's white reefs. The girl, who now squatted in plain view on the bridge, gave up her watch, squeezed between the shafts of metal topping the pontoon, and disappeared up the ragged embankment. Had the boat been willed there by her? A fit of coughing seized me and the ugly water inside jumped back into my nose and mouth. My slackened limbs reeled tight with the heat in my lungs and I doubled up. I spat until I could taste only spit.

Brambles intruded on the path, and it disappeared altogether for long stretches, only to reappear yards away as a white cleft in a sudden rise. The dense cashmere suit refused to dry and clung heavily to my thighs while at my ankles it came to hang in tatters, eaten by the thorns. I had to stop again and again to disengage an arm or leg from the long, crooked branches. Fine, frayed shreds of black were left to be lifted by the wind, I imagined, through the bushes and into the sky. The sun beat with tranquillity upon the flat rocks at the mountain's peak. Only there did I allow myself to rest. Randolph County basked quietly below, each dwelling standing out clearly a mile or more from the next on the thatchy, undulating sweep. I turned around. The river valley was a merciless black, the Riverhine itself glinting cold steel. No sunlight fell on that side of the mountain; a lid of upholstered lavender gray was tightening down. Oblivious to the mood of the neighboring valley, the great plain rolled, murmuring grass and sand, past its rickety spartan houses. Each house had its meager plot for seed-packet vegetables, now either dingy and rotting or scraped clean as a patch of shaven skin.

I found I was gazing at one tree in a soft valley of trees down the path to my immediate left. A light shone through its leaves, a beautiful blue light. The tree was a stunted oak; it must have been struck by lightening because it was shortened by half. One wide pale limb reached into the sky at a height double to that of the surrounding trees. The trees were new in that little valley. Perhaps a fire had spread from the oak to make the valley new. The limb of the oak was radiant with the blue light. The little valley was truly alive. A lump came into my throat: I knew she was there, by the oak.

The girl looked intently into my eyes, down at my naked feet, was absorbed by the black of my suit. Slowly, she came forward and stretched out her hand. I was astonished by this gesture and reached without thinking into my pocket where I found the frosted crystal of *Veronal-Nocturne*, which I placed in her hand. She smiled, turned, and ran away. At the entrance to the clearing, she stopped and gazed back at me. Poised there, the sun falling directly upon her, she held my gaze. She too was astonished, astonished that she had been so bold. Her fingers closed more tightly around the vial.

Along the base of the mountain ran a dirt road. At one end was a highway and at the other a dump. I followed the girl down the mountain to that puddly road. As we went, she never once glanced back. I hesitated before stepping into the road, lest I be seen by someone turning onto it from the highway, which was obscured by a shed. She ran in the direction of the dump, and I was tempted to follow, but just when I had determined how to trail her unseen, a pick-up truck emerged. The driver stopped when he came upon the girl and she climbed up into the cab with the silence of familiarity. The girl stared straight ahead as they passed. The truck lumbered up the gully onto the highway, snorting exhaust, and whirred off across the great plain. Stunned, I sat down in the weeds, clasped my feet like two worthless relics in my sweating hands, and wondered.

I would travel by night. I would find the pick-up truck. I would find the house in which the girl lived. I would look in each and every window for her. The rooms, set in the dark volumes of the house, would be yellow-orange with electric light; her hair would shine like polished brass. If the curtains were drawn, I would wait for the inhabitants to appear at their windows with the daylight.

It was a typical Randolph County house: wooden frame, two-story, solitary in a shorn field. One light shone in the kitchen. I'd lain over the warm hood of the pick-up truck watching until the metal had cooled. The boulder behind which I now crouched was silken with paint, and as the sky grew brighter, its red skin began to shine. All the big rocks in the yard, scattered like misshapen pool balls, were painted red or green. With the sun, they either vibrated in silhouette against the smart acid-green grass or melted into it.

With a crack, the back door opened and closed and the man left the house. He stood in the driveway for a long time, staring into space as if he'd forgotten something. Then the door of the pick-up creaked and thudded, the ignition grated, the engine responding with an onerous boom, and he was off, moist chocolatey dirt flying from his treads. With his departure, the house became invitingly vulnerable. But just when I'd gathered the courage to get up, the back door again cracked and a woman in a maroon housecoat appeared with a basket of wash. She bent and stretched beneath the line strung tight between two tall pipes, her nipples visible through her nightie. I assumed she was the girl's mother, but I was wrong: as it turns out, the woman was her Aunt Naomi, the girl's legal guardian.*

---

* Since the Wurtzheim Clinic was founded in June of 1932, all of the local newspapers have been kept and filed. The head nurse, Mrs Lathrop, is a qualified librarian. She explained to me that the countless racks of brittle sheets are essential to the institution for evidentiary purposes, that she has herself compiled reports too numerous to count on patients incapable of recalling the public events of their lives. Using the clinic's files, I've been able to composite a fairly accurate picture of Dorothy Belmar's life and family, for that was in fact the girl's name, Dorothy Belmar. I'd passed over the tractor tire partially buried at the end of the lane, 'Belmar Road' lettered on it with white paint, without attaching any real significance to the name: the girl was Virginnia's spiritual descendent, that was all I knew or cared to know. Dorothy Belmar's mother, Constance, had been decapitated in an automobile accident. Her father, one Parker Belmar, lay permanently comatose in the Veterans' Hospital at Boxington, his body cauterized from the waist down in the

Without make-up, Aunt Naomi's face was one of those faces that doesn't quite exist. Her mahogany hair was bobby-pinned in flat swirls on the top of her head while long wisps, brushed behind her ears, fell in loops about her neck and shoulders. The slight breeze carried the wisps back across her cheeks, and she stopped now and then to retwine them around her ears. Near her slippered feet, miscellaneous car parts suggested the organs of a recently slaughtered animal strewn about the grassless patches for the dogs. The slaughtered animal itself, a rusted-out sedan turned a chalky iridescent blue by the sun, hovered on its axles on four stacks of cinder blocks several yards away. Perfecting the desolate surrealism of this scene, with Aunt Naomi at its center, was the robot-like presence of an electrical tower casting its centurion shadow over the roof of the house, others ranging in perspective across the great plain and through the mountain pass. When Aunt Naomi reached the near end of the clothesline and turned to begin filling a second

---

same wreck. An empty gin bottle was found wedded by the intense heat to the steering wheel. Constance Belmar's body was found twenty-five yards from the car in a field. Her head was found amongst the char-bedded springs of the backseat. Theirs was a sad but romantic story. Pictures of both were printed side by side on the front page of the New Caledonia Star when Parker Belmar died, he in his Army dress uniform decorated with two Purple Hearts and she in the hideously expensive wedding dress begrudgingly paid for by her rich daddy. Belmar had taken Mr and Mrs Esterbrooke's lovely daughter away to live in a state of financial oblivion on the great scrubby plain, and indeed that was how they lived until the end. Although Parker Belmar remained a handsome nobody, but for his medals, and Constance a ravishingly dreary memory for all who had known her before she'd made her dreadful mistake, they must have stayed tumultuously in love, for their short life together, fourteen years married, appears to have been a succession of quarrels and reconciliations punctuated by haphazard entanglements with the law. From this wild, undignified union had come Dorothy. With Dorothy, Naomi Belmar Bickle had inherited the house. They lived with Aunt Naomi's second husband, called Leonard Ruth. But Aunt Naomi suffered, the custody of her three children having been awarded to her ex-husband's mother.

line, I dashed for the porch. I found the porch fanned completely around the building. There it hung precariously over the
escarpment of a bituminous excavation. The vast pit was not
only an eyesore but a menace, its depths populated by more
derelict cars, their crumpled jaws yawning ragged metal and
pulverized glass. I crept onto the porch. Precautionary screen-
ing masked the view, giving it an appropriately dingy tone.
The paint on the handrail was blistered and warm. To the left
of the screendoor was a window. On the wall between, a Penn-
zoil thermometer identical to the one at the Riverhine Hotel
swung noiselessly on a rubber-coated hook. Keeping my face
flush with the window frame, I peered through the grime-
speckled panes. A taxidermied shark hung above a couch on
which the girl was lying naked. Her eyes were closed tightly, as
though she found the sunlight streaking her face bothersome,
but I realized her brow was furrowed with concentration. She
was concentrating on another source of heat, the room's
swimming silence light-years away.

The sun fell harder on the window, warming my face, and
the temperature climbed in the thermometer by my hand. The
fingers of the other hand, I realized, breaking from my
thoughtless staring, had been intermittently brushing the in-
seam of my trousers, ridged with the thickening inside. The
shape of her mouth shifted ceaselessly as she worked, and her
nostrils flared. Her luxuriantly thick brows pinched harder and
her face took on the look of sublime, suffering apprehension.
She hunched up, her shoulders lifted by an invisible tidewater,
her thighs suddenly buoyant.

"Can I help you?" asked Aunt Naomi.

Turning toward the voice, the thermometer coming away
from the wall in my hand, I stammered, "My . . . I . . ."

I should have been prepared. I should have simply turned
and said, sedately, "Hello, I'm somebody or other, and I was
wondering if, etc., etc." But no, instead I danced about on my
filthy naked feet grappling with the thermometer as if her question, so calmly and naturally put, had triggered some mecha-

nism inside me gone haywire. And although she plainly saw my nervousness, embodied as it was in a chattering fit of agitation, she continued to regard me without the slightest bit of wariness. When the lurker on her porch had twitched the thermometer back onto its hook and had managed to still himself by clamping his arms to his sides, Aunt Naomi smiled reassuringly and asked once again, "Can I help you?"

"I'm sorry. Yes. I was just—I don't know where I am, if I'm headed in the right direction. I'm trying to get to Ironstone, but I just don't know." She listened patiently, waiting for me to finish my rambling, but rather than gazing into my eyes, she was looking at my feet, so I added, "Oh, I know, yes, someone must have stolen them at the train station, where I was obliged to sleep last—I mean, two nights ago. I would have bought other ones, used ones, or new ones, but they must have taken my money too because I don't have any. It was in my jacket pocket. Stupid, I know, I should have kept it hidden, but, you know."

Then I found myself presenting to Aunt Naomi a question of an extremely tangential nature, in fact so tangential that she came to eye me with bald-faced suspicion.

"What," I asked, "is this confounding preoccupation with historical dates that so paralyzes the learning process in the parochial schools of this country?"

Aunt Naomi pressed her hand to the flimsy azure stuff gathered over her bosom, pulled the housecoat closed, and squinted at me.

"If you're lost, Route 73 heads east and west. Out that way—" She pointed over her shoulder vaguely in the direction of the highway. "When you're out there, Luriatown's to the left and Ironstone's to the right. Couldn't be simpler. If you're lost—well, I ain't got a telephone."

A pick-up truck came dusting up the lane, a brown one with gray fenders and a wooden storage cabinet built over the bed. Ignoring me, Aunt Naomi walked expectantly over to the latched gate at the driveway end of the porch and, resting her hands lightly on the top rail where it nestled into her hips, waited on tiptoe to see through the dust. The red and green boulders marked her harbor, the maroon housecoat the rouleau of her lighthouse. Silvery rays darted about her head as she plucked the pins from her hair, now certain of her caller. She raced by me into the house, leaving the door ajar. I watched as the girl, clutching her bathrobe about her, disappeared down the hallway. I could hear Aunt Naomi rustling about in the kitchen, and I could see the driver of the truck clearly now as he turned off the driveway to cut across the yard and park behind the house, apparently out of sight from the highway.

I'd hoped to pass the night in the gray plush of an extinct La-Salle limousine at the bottom of the pit, but it didn't work: as I tossed and turned, the seat quickly became a topographical disaster of irksome jutting springs and effluxes of fetid cotton stuffing, and sleep never came. I decided to have another look into the house, left the car's moldy interior, scurried out of the pit, and took up a position behind my favorite boulder. Well past midnight—I was certain—and yet several lights still burned. Loud voices came from the porch. The screendoor slammed and I distinctly heard a man, Leonard Ruth, swearing bitterly. He next erupted in the kitchen. I ran the length of the house, past several unlit rooms, to the edge of the pit where I found a window with a clear view through the house into the kitchen. Leonard Ruth appeared smaller this way, but nearly whole, with just his feet blocked by the top of a small table in the room directly before me. And Aunt Naomi could be seen shifting before the sink, her back turned indignantly to him. There in the room through which I looked into the kitchen was a bed, and on the bed lay the girl, trying to sleep. The dim light in the hallway beyond sent a diagonal shaft over her uncovered form, the girl's legs suddenly very white as she turned over. I went right up to the window and stayed there. The window had one big upper and one big lower pane, and the lower was broken, its cracks mended with black electrician's tape. The cracks were concentrated at the bottom, where someone had brushed yellow and blue and red paint onto the shiny surfaces between the tracks of tape to create the effect of a stained-glass window.

The girl drew herself up into a knot. The soiled nightie she wore barely covered her buttocks. It was several sizes too small. As I glanced from her nakedness to Leonard Ruth, with his powerful hirsute shoulders, swaying over Aunt Naomi, this sad deprivation became more and more ominous. I saw what the future held for Dorothy Belmar, and it was worse than nothing. Yes, I saw Dorothy Belmar's future clearly, and all at once.

Leonard Ruth shouted, "Me? I couldn't giva fuck?"

To which Aunt Naomi responded, "Don't use that filthy language to me, Leonard. Just don't."

"Fuck, fuck, fuck, and fuck your lousy mother too!" His singsong was working on her, and he knew it; and he kept it up, softly and sweetly now. "I got that much fuckin' concern for you and your fuckin' kids."

"Oh God, why don't you just leave the kids out of it?"

"Bet they'd like to know about their lousy fuckin' mother—heh, Naomi? Whatya say, Naomi—whatya say? Right. So why in the hell should I hafta clean up Bickle's mess? Why in the hell should I, it's your fuckin' mess, you fuckin' lousy bitch."

Aunt Naomi turned and screamed, talons reaching: "I said, shut your filthy mouth, Leonard! Now shut Dorothy's door, like I told you before! If you're gonna open your filthy mouth, then shut her door."

"Shut the kid's door? Bullshit!"

He had her by the wrists. They struggled for a moment—then suddenly she was still, and so was he. She yanked her hands free and stepped back. Hands on hips, she looked him up and down. Leonard Ruth wasn't infuriated by her vacuous staring eyes and lazily drooping body. He was excited by them. His was an extremely sexual form of frustration.

Leonard Ruth glowered by the stove, toying with a jelly

glass. Aunt Naomi rocked gently from side to side on a stool. She rose wearily and went shuffling by him. Just as she passed him, he slapped the jelly glass against the back of her neck. The glass broke over firm muscle. It dropped from his hand to the floor. It hit loudly, breaking again. As if stung by an insect, she brushed away the pieces of glass lodged in her skin. Now her blood flowed. Dorothy Belmar was sitting up in her bed, craning her neck to see through the hallway and into the kitchen, but she couldn't. Aunt Naomi's bared teeth bit down on the word 'bastard.' The girl again leaned reluctantly into the light. No sound came from the kitchen. Scarlet ran along Aunt Naomi's arm and dripped from her elbow into the sink. The girl slowly lay back on the bed, her naked belly pulsing.

I spun from Dorothy's window to the next. Crooked smile fixed in place, Aunt Naomi wove into the dank cavern, junk clinging to every available surface, that was their bedroom. The washcloth Aunt Naomi had pressed to her neck was rapidly darkening. I spun back to Dorothy's window. Leonard Ruth teetered on his heels as he looked down into the bloody sink, his face blackened by shadow. His stocky torso seemed diminished by the violence. An unexpected flourish of activity dazzled in the doorway as Aunt Naomi went by, changing from her bloodstained housecoat into a fluid satiny robe as she did. An instant later she veered back across the hallway. Orange mercurochrome flashed around her collar against the kitchen's distant fluorescent blue. The bedroom door slammed. Leonard Ruth came into the passage and stared at the door. He tried the knob. The door was locked. He turned into the girl's room and just stood there. Now I could hear Aunt Naomi softly whimpering. Leonard Ruth stood staring stupidly at Dorothy Belmar's naked belly.

The girl rolled over, her buttocks once again opalescent, but now in the shadow of the hulking man in his sleeveless undershirt. Breathing shallowly, he moved closer to the bed. Leonard Ruth leaned over, stretched out one big hand, and lay it down upon Dorothy Belmar's buttocks. He remained immobile, staring dumbly down, the hand upon her crude and dead as a broken branch. Pipes clanked in the basement as the boiler rumbled on, and Leonard Ruth sat down on the bed. I watched helplessly as he lifted his hand from her and unzipped his fly. Sweat began to pour from me. One arm hanging limp so that his hand rested on the floor, Aunt Naomi's husband squeezed his penis, the knob of it big as a baby's head, with the other. A string of spit fell from his mouth to be worked along the shaft. All the while he stared down with glazed eyes at Dorothy Belmar's nakedness.

My elbow hit the window. Glass smashed over the sill and fell into the room. In that moment, the molester was on his hands and knees on the floor. He poked his snout qualmishly into the draft and winced as he moved over the fragments to the window. I dove headlong into the pit. Risen in terror, the starlings that nested in the rusting cars volleyed over me in the orchid-blue sky. I drove my face into the damp black dirt. I pounded my brow with weak fists. I tore at my guts with useless fingers, blood glossing the metal shapes around me.

As I lay in the LaSalle, my sleeve growing heavier with my blood, I sought to distract myself from my worsening predicament. All around the ragged hole in which the car had been dumped lay Randolph County. This November the plain was unseasonably warm, like a tropical savanna, its stillness humid and close. The waterless days were yet to begin. Come January the heavens would clear and remain clear, the occasional stringy cloud strummed by only the driest wind. The grass would quickly turn to straw. The snows would blow in in late March and drift over the vast basin, caught as the heat was now caught, until the first spell of spring turned the fields to marshes.

I remembered Aunt Naomi coming out onto the porch that morning, her hair snapping with static electricity as she whisked a big plastic comb through it. And I remembered Dorothy Belmar, her hair so blonde as to appear gaseous in the dazzling sunlight, lying on the faded sofa below the stuffed shark, its awful gray mass a vision of purgatorial inertia. Onto the tattered imitation Persian carpet she'd dropped her bathrobe, its sash, serpentine and cerulean blue, dangling by her red-flecked toes. I'd wondered what song was playing in her head as she'd swung her leg slowly away from the sofa and back—away and back, away and back. I'd closed my mouth, which had hung open as I'd seen young Raimund's do, seeping moisture. I'd closed it and swallowed hard, but still the moisture had come. She'd then placed one foot over the other, her fingers commencing their entrancing business, and tensed her thighs. Reminding me of Lydie Fay, she'd glanced down at her breasts, rising with the pressure of her arms. My pulse had beaten louder and louder in my ears, crisp cold air biting into their soft shells. She'd then touched herself with just one finger, then softly brushed her palm over the wispy swell above.

A lead slug shot across the rue Charlemagne, ripped through the canvas panel advertising throat spray that hid the piano-tuner's cracked front window, and embedded itself hotly in one of the boards bracing the panel from behind. The canvas vibrated violently, causing the bosomy warbling ingenue gracing the tableau to shudder with corseted stiffness. The bullet could only have been meant for me; it had to be Desmanche's. Like an angry red atom, the point of entry near the bosomy ingenue's collarbone pulsed in the night. There was a pinging and a splintering as the slug threw its gears into reverse and whirred back through the canvas to hang in a glowing ingot over the street about a yard from the tableau's surface. The slug commenced lodging and dislodging itself in the board, enlarging the hole in the ingenue's breast. The wood continued to splinter behind the canvas until it erupted about the smoking wound, tearing the bosomy warbling ingenue's flesh apart.

I sat slumped in the LaSalle at the bottom of the pit, my lacerated arm cradled in the curve of the steering wheel, and stared blindly at the filthy windshield. Dawn colored the earth as Dorothy Belmar stood on the edge of the pit looking at herself in a small bright gold compact, her white anklets and shiny black maryjanes unsuited to the new womanliness of her legs. Her face, round and smooth and pretty as those of the little ladies scurrying through the rain in Hokusai's Kyoto, caught the light of the waxing moon. Her tongue darted between her lips to moisten the rouge, but its bitterness made her wince. She snapped the compact shut without another thought and dropped it into her apron pocket. Crouching as she had by the river, she surveyed the pit, inspecting each derelict car as though it were a prized butterfly mounted on a pin.

Dorothy Belmar sauntered away from the pit. I followed. Outside the car I found puddles of ink, the stretch between me and the edge of the pit a breeding conflux of glassy pools. A yellow cardboard box and one emerald gumdrop lay in the ink at my bruised feet. I wondered how I was to face her again, looking as I did. The coal-soot cashmere was dull as tarpaper, besmirched with the river's scum, in rags at my pagan feet. And still the blood continued to flow along my arm and into my hand. Oh Uncle Deitrich, if only you could see me now, I laughed, mirthlessly. And then, in an instant, I knew it didn't matter what spoiled cloth I wore. I knew nothing mattered to her but the fact of my existence. Joy swelled in my chest and I reached into the sky and fashioned the passing clouds into likenesses of Dorothy Belmar and me strolling by the bluest sea, wading together into the water, swimming side by side. Morning would come.

Handful after handful of sun-warmed rainwater—the rainwater lay in the dish of a dented finder in the pit—rinsed the dried blood from my wounds. My arm had plunged down on the taped glass at the bottom of Dorothy Belmar's window, the resulting slivers penetrating the soft cashmere and thence penetrating the bone. The largest gash, the flesh sliced too wide to knit, continued to leak a pinkish fluid. Obviously, I needed proper medical care—antiseptic lotion, stitches, and the like—but this never occurred to me. Instead I fastened on Virginnia and the love with which she had tended my head wound at Euphrosinia. The rainwater surfeited the black slits, like so many city streets on a map, while the gash itself began to turn yellow. It was no good. And then I recalled Lester telling me that during the Revolutionary War the Lenilenape Indians had healed many a Prussian mercenary by packing the unsuturable wounds with mud and ground herbs. Thank you, Lester, you were good for something after all. For me, a grouting of mud alone would have to do.

Tearing my shirt and knotting it around a disconnected engine rod, I fashioned a tourniquet to lessen the pinkish flow. Bent low, I ran along the drainage ditch to the culvert under the highway, where I hoped to find enough water to make mud. The mud trembled in the air as it entered the gash to lie against the bone inside. There in the culvert, my trousers wet about my ankles, I squatted and bathed my genitals. I returned exhausted to the LaSalle intending to sleep, but my hatred for Leonard Ruth and, increasingly by association, Aunt Naomi, dominated my thoughts, and I found myself transported—over Luriatown, upon a current of cold air.

By propelling myself ahead of them a few yards and then hovering, I could observe Aunt Naomi and Leonard Ruth below their bobbing umbrella as they hurried along Tulip Avenue. They both were bundled in expensive cloth. Why, Leonard even had his coat draped over his shoulders like an Italian count! I couldn't imagine where they were going, but they couldn't have been going very far in such a downpour. As usual, they were at odds, arguing as they went. The cars parked along the street, bulbous fenders glistening, were all bedecked with tiny American flags. Predictably, Leonard Ruth halted, tore at Aunt Naomi's sleeve, and knocked the umbrella from her hand. Immediately their faces, savagely contorted in the storm's yellowish light, were streaked with rain and gleaming. It was a ghastly spectacle. Determined to leave him standing alone and humiliated, Aunt Naomi swung furiously around, knocking Leonard Ruth's coat to the wet pavement. He grimaced and swore. A Packard sedan entered Tulip Avenue from

Oriole Street. At the speed the Packard was going, Oriole's steepness and slipperiness made it impossible to brake properly, and the big sedan slid across the intersection. Its tires thudded against the curbing and its lights went off.

"Hear that?" said Lester to Lydie Fay. "That's the lead from the switch sparking against the manifold or whatever."

"I told you. Those lights go—"

"Yea, flickering. I know, it's loose," whined Lester. "So I'm not the sort of mechanically-minded guy who makes a mental note to take the car to the garage all the time — so what?"

"Well, you could say it's too late, and right in the middle of a storm, and going to lunch," murmured Lydie Fay, glancing down the street at the altercation between Leonard Ruth and Aunt Naomi. "Those people are fighting," she said bluntly, turning to her husband.

"It's none of our fucking business," said Lester, and threw the Packard into gear.

The man Lester saw lurching out from between parked cars as the Packard sped on was not the man Leonard Ruth saw himself to be at that moment in his fine suit. For Lester, the man in the middle of the street was a drunken wretch in wasted grays laughing idiotically to himself, nothing more than a carcass of cirrhotic human meat with a grotesque smile painted on.

"Nothing I can do—the brakes are locked," said Lester. "I'm gonna hit him, yes?"

"And he's as big as a cow," observed Lydie Fay.

Bent double, Leonard Ruth's head met the chrome grille with a walloping thunk. Lester, having taken his foot from the brake pedal, sailed on.

Aunt Naomi's expression was one of patrician calm. She didn't care to view her husband's remains. What could be more vulgar? She picked up the umbrella and went on. Below me on Tulip Avenue, his greasy hair soaking in blood, sprawled Leonard Ruth. Having thusly inherited his fortune, Aunt Naomi never returned to Belmar Road. Dorothy and I decided to keep the house, for the time being. Tonight we would spend our first night together, alone at last, our love beaming its light over that dismal plain in Randolph County.

Light shone through the keyhole. We lay together, Dorothy and I, in our warm bed in the crooked wooden house by the pit at the end of the rocky lane. We would be drawn together forever, ourselves becoming our flesh becoming ourselves. Luminous particles, reaching into the darkness, spun over the walls, under the bed, finally to fall like the soft breath of the sea upon us.

"Your wave is sweeping over me," she whispered, "bringing you in, into my belly, filling me so wonderfully full."

"Our wave," I sobbed into her golden hair, "please, only our wave . . ."

"Now you're here," she said, "inside me . . . Verdon, fill me so full, so full with your love . . . now that you're here . . ."

But I wasn't. I was hunched in the LaSalle, my forehead pressed to the dashboard, crying.

Blond ringlets all radiant, Dorothy Belmar stood on the sun-drenched porch holding a bottle of milk. Milk glistened on her upper lip. Smiling, she held the bottle out to me. But there was a whole sky of spurned clouds between us, and they were buffeting me backwards in a whirling tide. Daintily teasing the slick neck with wet fingers, she let the bottle's full weight slip into her palm again and again. What mischief played on that smiling mouth. If she let it, the bottle would drop and break on the steps. Little did she know how much I needed that milk. Again and again the bottle slipped by its neck through her wet fingers. The bottle began its fall. The muscles about my rectum contracted. The milk flooded, and was suspended, from the glinting rim. My rectum throbbed as the embolism lodged in my guts passed from me. The bottle plummeted all the way to the very bottom step to spin on its side in the sun. The wetness streamed down the backs of my thighs. Dorothy Belmar picked up the bottle and drank what was left. Squatting on the steps, she trailed her fingers in the milk lingering on the dry wood, then, lowering her head, blew the white puddle into the thirsty weeds. With this innocent gesture, the house rising over her began to burn in the incinerator behind my eyes.

The great yellow mass of the schoolbus eclipsed the sun. It roared, idling, over me as I pressed myself into the gully, regaining its jaunty character only when it went round the bend well in the distance. Leonard Ruth's truck remained where he'd left it the evening before. I hadn't any guarantee that Aunt Naomi and her husband were still asleep, but my intuition was that they were. Maybe she'd kept the bedroom door locked all night and he'd had to sleep on the couch. It didn't really matter where they were sleeping; if the fire spread quickly enough, from the four walls inward, they would be trapped.

The girl's nearness had bewildered me. I'd thought of her breasts lined with the twisted sheets as she'd risen that morning, of her cheeks still flushed with sleep, of her slender hand reaching to switch on the porcelain lamp by her bed to examine the vial of *Veronal-Nocturne*. And I'd wondered if it was rage I was meant to feel; if it was, then perhaps I had the mettle to endure my ordeal, for I was raging inside with contempt for the brutality I saw everywhere. It was no wonder Englehard had succumbed to Frederic's vision of a world demonically unhinged, a world guided by the evil stupidity of gluttonous human beings in all kinds of sophisticated and unsophisticated guises. Dorothy Belmar was not meant to suffer such evil stupidity. When she stepped from the bus that afternoon she would find nothing but quiet, the great rolling plain suddenly less encumbered—nothing but quiet, and sweet-smelling ashes.

The gas can in Leonard Ruth's truck was full. It was exhausting work lugging the thing around the house with only one good arm, but its wooden handle swiveled loosely on a wire loop, like a wire hanger, and pouring was simply a matter of tipping the can's weight off-center, which I could easily manage with my damaged arm. However, the emptier the can, the higher I had to lift, and the more painful it became. In the end, I had to resort to awkwardly flinging the gasoline against the house with my left hand, using the only container I could find—a child's watering can. I saturated each window and door and everything around them. Not once did I hear a sound in the house; it was as if they were already dead. Leonard Ruth was a cigar smoker, and there were partially used books of matches all over the pick-up's filthy seat and floor.

The fire thundered above me as I lay in the pit waiting. The porch flew in huge flaming hunks across the sky, and the wind howled. The electrical cables fell from the tower and into the pit, screeching and sizzling and shooting melted black rubber over the abandoned cars as they twisted and leapt like eels on hot stones. Some of the cars in the pit had caught fire with the marauding blazing debris, and I worried that they might still have gas in their tanks and explode. But just as I was envisioning myself penetrated by shards of metal and pieces of glass, or blown to bits to be eaten by the crows, Dorothy's voice came singing into me. I knew she was somewhere above me, waiting for me, as I'd been waiting for her. Once again she was singing silently into me. I climbed out of the pit. The burning house completely dominated the landscape. Even the steel legs of the electrical tower glowed with its heat. There, on the porch, in a pocket of cold silence, stood the geisha. Her face was powdered white and her mouth painted blood-red in the shape of two merging droplets. Clouds of blackness rolled about her head, away from her face, and brightly colored sticks sparkled there, like shooting stars. She held a fan folded against the pale green silk at her breast. She didn't move; she only looked, into me. Then she stiffened as the air around her was all at once boiling. The boiling air, gushing from the center of the inferno, ripped her garment from her back, outwards, as if by gigantic hands. It fell in smoldering black sheets over her naked hips. Her sleeves unfurled along her arms and fell in charred bracelets from her wrists. In her eyes, the doomed seconds meant nothing. She stood defiantly pale and straight as a curtain of blinding light rose behind her, and the house, in one mammoth wave of nonsensical matter, was no more. Her pocket of cold silence was the threshold of eternity. Dorothy Belmar walked by me in flames, into the pit.

Ironstone Reporter, November 21st, 1943

NAOMI RUTH, Belmar Road, Ironstone. Died in fire at home on November 12th, aged 29. Beloved daughter of Mr. & Mrs. Harry Belmar of Clarenceburg, wife of the late Robert L. Bickle Sr. Mrs. Ruth is survived by her second husband, Leonard, and her three children: Doris, Dorian, and Robert Bickle Jr.

DOROTHY BELMAR, Belmar Road, Ironstone. Died in fire at home on November 12th, aged 12. Much loved daughter of the late Constance Esterbrooke Belmar and Lieutenant Commander Parker Belmar. Cherished granddaughter of Harry and Violet Belmar.

Services were held at St. James Episcopal Church, Clarenceburg, on November 19th.

1984

From THE MIRACLE OF FONTANA'S MONKEY
Chapter 5

Nice & Marseilles 1934

Jerome and Violette Desroches were meeting at last. Lunch had been arranged, naturally, by their employer. De Hauteville, while giving Jerome protracted instructions on how he should behave when in the presence of his leading lady, had confessed, with hypocritical smuttiness, to cherishing the scent of *Tati* on his genitals. In fact, he cherished it so much, he said, that Dudu had recently objected to its presence in their life.

"It's very long and very smooth," said Violette to Jerome. "And if you've been wondering if he's a Jew, he's not."

"It hadn't crossed my mind," said Jerome, and immediately began weighing those attributes of de Hauteville's that might very well be Jewish against those that might very well be not.

He now glanced from the oysters hovering on their plateau of ice to Violette, who quite forcefully held his gaze. Her eyes *were* huge, with irises of the palest glimmering purple. Jerome couldn't help but stare. It was as if, pupils permanently dilated, she were in a state of constant wonderment. But her smile told another story. It was lascivious. She was like a perfectly smooth, perfectly formed female demon. Once, in the fragrant shadows of a Japanese import shop, Jerome had come upon a doll—he had even held it very briefly with trembling adolescent fingers—its tiny breasts apparent beneath its miniature silk kimono. Eyes round and glistening as two droplets of ink, lips smiling and red, as if drawn with a scalpel, the doll had provoked a strange and disquieting response in him: he had stolen it, strolled out into the street, and crushed its dainty head under his heel.

"You're Jewish, aren't you?" Violette playfully insisted, fingering the end, squared and nubbly, of his argyle tie.

"Well, I'd have to be, wouldn't I?"

She looked up at him uncomprehendingly.

"How else could I play our big love scene with any credibility?" Jerome remained unconvinced of the value of such coarse humour.

"It's not *that* kind of picture, is it?" Of course she was kidding too.

Jerome placed another oyster on her plate. Violette raised the shell to her lips and sucked. The oyster resided there, upon her tongue, for a moment before slipping without injury down her throat.

"Hugo was a postal clerk," stated Jerome, glumly.

"So?"

"I don't much like the idea of portraying Jesus as something Hugo's been."

"Pity."

Jerome wondered if anyone could truly be so lacking in empathy. He decided it would be best to draw the conversation back to her. "Hugo gave me a rather fanciful rendition of your first meeting."

"There really wasn't much to it. I was having lunch at the hotel one day with Count Lazovsky when Hugo came over to say hello."

"He didn't tell me you were having lunch with the Count."

"I wasn't having *only* lunch with him."

"Oh."

"You're not jealous?"

"Why should I be jealous?"

"Men like to think I belong to them."

Modesty clearly not on her agenda that afternoon, Violette opened her mouth and lolled her tongue between her teeth, signalling the desire for another oyster. Jerome couldn't help but think of Hugo de Hauteville at that moment: how he would have savoured her performance, her flawless neck lightly flushed and pulsing, her eyes narrowed, her mouth gleaming wetly, her small but fruity breasts mounded over her bodice, cut like the ruffled sides of a candy-box. But Jerome found it all so very predictable.

As he put another oyster on her plate, she caught his free hand and lowered it under the table where it served to remind them, his fingers finding a hidden mouth that also wanted to be fed, that each had best consider a main course before the kitchen closed for the afternoon.

"I seldom see the Count anymore," Violette assured him.

"I doubt the Count would want to risk seeing you."

"I said *seldom*." She glanced at the bottle of champagne in its silver bucket—it was nearly empty. "Lady Duckworth never took me seriously anyway, not until Hugo cast me in the role of Tati."

"How do you know she takes you seriously now?"

"I don't. But I do know she assumes I'll be spending considerably less time with her precious Sergei—because Hugo's so possessive himself." Violette cast her smile in the direction of a table nearby, challenging the woman seated there to keep staring at her. "Hugo's not much of a man, but he is rather nice."

"He's obliged to be nice." Jerome withdrew his hand from the soft small place and signalled for the waiter to bring another bottle.

"I was always told gentlemen liked pathological sex," said Violette, stretching her arms and feigning to stifle a yawn.

"By whom?"

"By the Count."

"That's interesting."

It was just then that a very unkempt *clochard* strode by the restaurant waving a newspaper wildly in the air.

"Look there—outside in the street!" exclaimed Jerome. "There he is!"

"*Who?*" Violette remonstrated, more annoyed than startled by his behaviour.

"The man's in a kind of ecstasy ..."

"Perhaps he's swatting flies," suggested Violette, reaching for a cigarette.

"But don't you see—there's a photograph of Joey on the front page."

Now Violette looked more closely at Jerome, who was staring out into the sunstruck street, oblivious to her wants. She held up her unlit cigarette, pouted, and inquired indignantly, "Who's Joey?"

The anemones stood in a porcelain Chinese pot before the

window. The lace curtain, tiny pom-poms along its edges, had been drawn back to let in the breeze. Although the sea was blocked from view by the buildings along the Rue St Säens, the sky beyond the window was alive with its rectifying brilliance. Over the pale yellow walls of the nursery were looped innumerable magenta peonies, some faded to pink, the wallpaper itself powdery with age. In a slightly darker yellow, a volume of the thoughts of Pascal rested on the table before the window. The table, which was draped in white linen, also held a bowl of lemons. The bowl was the colour of old ivory. The crib was also white, but its white was as fresh as the lemons were yellow.

There was a harmony to this arrangement that Joey greatly appreciated. He continued to admire the scene as he finished his cigarette, his other hand resting on Raphaela's delectable bottom. Raphaela slept peacefully beside him. Glancing down, Joey noted the woman's purse he had stolen while leaving the park, which lay by his lover's hip. This touch of black, glossy but muted and not quite round, was the single element, he concluded, that gave this fine interior its mystery.

Raphaela's lips puckered as she slept, and a crystalline bubble, pure as the purest spring water, eased out between them. Joey leaned over and kissed the bubble away. As he did, he tasted, regretfully, the exquisite sweetness of her being.

From the sill, another still-life was conjured, the crib hovering perfectly at the top of the arrangement. Joey rose on his toes to glimpse Raphaela one last time before descending into the street and retracing his steps back through the dust of Marseilles to the sanctuary of the Parc Borély.

As had been agreed beforehand, Jerome returned to the Negresco after his luncheon with Violette to make a full report to his employer. But before he could even say how much they had enjoyed themselves, de Hauteville was off and running.

"It wouldn't be good for your concentration," he said. "On the other hand, once you've had her, she'll be utterly irresistible to you, and this will, undoubtedly, read quite clearly and effectively on the screen."

"Only in the close-ups, I would imagine," Jerome conjectured.

"But desire is best communicated by one's total—what?—*demeanour*. It should be evident even in one's stride," de Hauteville declared, with satisfaction.

"I'll have to work on that," said Jerome. He then got up and paced to the far side of the room and back. "What do you think?"

"Not bad—for a first attempt." De Hauteville glanced at himself in the mirror over the settee on which Jerome had been sitting and nodded in agreement with himself.

Always delighted by his own paradoxical nature and the unselfish joy he took in making his friends' hearts beat a little faster, Hugo de Hauteville gave in to glorious compulsion. Savouring the irony, he telephoned Violette—with Jerome standing right there next to him—to warn her never to visit the actor's rooms. Lombardi, he said, was a young man without conscience, who would certainly take advantage of her without sufficient recompense. For Jerome, it was a hurtful kind of joking. But de Hauteville's callow behaviour was of no matter, because Violette and Jerome had already agreed to meet that evening—at his flat on St. Rita's Apron.

"I know what it is to die," said Jerome to the woman standing next to him at the bar, her tiny purple hat clinging to the side of her head like a sticky candy.

"Do tell," said the woman. Her spurious aristocratic tone was utterly at odds with what Jerome knew intuitively to be her sympathetic nature.

"The trees overhanging the path were black, quite black. The path, I sensed, led to the place where I belong, where I am truly myself, without fear, without guilt or remorse."

Jerome glanced at the woman, wondering if she knew he was performing.

She said nothing.

"It was this *distance* I wished so desperately to attain. The air in which I stood was a lustrous filmy grey, and the black trees, the path penetrating their bower, were sublime, unnervingly sublime."

Now he would use his eyes, imploring, losing sight of all reason, to draw her in, until she literally melted into him, as so many had done in the darkened depths of the theatre.

"I was overcome by a feeling of helplessness, a failing in the limbs that surely extended from my very soul. My body, I knew, was relinquishing its presence in the world." If only I can bring this intensity to my rendering of Victor Didot, Jerome prayed silently. "As the trees grew blacker and the silvery air came to permeate my being, my way along the path became impossible. This was to be my ultimate limitation, my undoing. And the trees grew blacker still."

The woman was staring, he knew, through the shaggy limbs of those black trees at a terrible, terrible image of herself.

"No longer was I capable of any action, and my heart grew sad, with regret. But then my heart grew sadder still, with its passing into the enveloping atmosphere." Jerome gasped a little. He couldn't help it, he was so moved. "The luminous air shone into me, and my mind, retreating into my soul, yearned for my heart to be still, murmuring, evermore softly, slow... slow... slow..."

The woman and Jerome shared a long quiet moment. Finally, her lower lip trembling, the woman said, "A place where I too might belong."

Jerome put some money on the bar—enough to pay for his last drink and for several more for the woman, for whom he knew the night would be endless—and walked out into the street.

Dusk was shimmering on the walls of the buildings, turning the yellow plaster a peculiarly roseate hue of pale green. Farther along, at the corner, was another bar. It cast its fanning aura of orange over the tables, their white cloths like smouldering discs of sulphur. Jerome wondered what Violette would think of his meagre rooms with their view of the ordinary little chapel on the square. He wished he didn't feel quite so anxious about being altogether alone with her, and stupidly wished he hadn't refused the chloral his pal Delphine had offered to send from Paris. The entire enterprise, and especially the content of

Mr. Didot, suddenly struck Jerome as unworthy. He saw himself floating just blocks away in the bay, the morning sun glancing over his lifeless upturned eyeballs and grimacing teeth, and he saw this same image looming in monotone over an audience held captive by the overwhelming reality of what they saw on the screen before them.

"But I'm not a martyr," he snorted, "I'm a fool. From what infestation of the soul do I suffer to be so bereft of conscience? Somewhere, at this very moment, a dying child is gazing beseechingly upon Christ's atrocious wounds. But how could anyone, especially a dying child, find comfort in Christ's suffering?" Overcome by a dreadful queasiness, Jerome walked on.

At the kiosk, he stared down at several newspapers laid out one on top of the other, each with its name and banner headline showing. Closest to him, at about the middle of *Le Monde's* front page, its contents slipping round the fold, was an item which read:

MONKEY INFLAMES MARSEILLES POLICE

Unprecedented allegations of bestiality are being brought by sixteen married couples and one widower against Reynolds Fontana, the British society columnist, for sexual violation of their infant daughters by his pet monkey. Three of the families claimed their daughters, the oldest fourteen months, were impregnated. Medical examiners have confirmed these claims without explanation. In a contretemps requiring public apology, the monkey, which was to be destroyed, an action halted by an injunction brought by Mr. Fontana, vanished from its cage in the...

(here Jerome turned the newspaper over and read on)

Borély Gardens on the weekend. Police guarding the cage are uncertain as to how and when the animal escaped. Mr. Fontana is seeking a full investigation of the matter.

"It does put my particular quandary into perspective," said Jerome, as he flipped the paper back over and neatly aligned it with the others.

"How's that?" asked the tobacconist, reaching out to re-align the entire row of newspapers.

"The miracle of Fontana's monkey," said Jerome, holding the man's gaze.

The tobacconist raised his eyebrows, communicating nothing. Jerome smiled, feeling much better, and walked off in the direction of the nearest taxi stand.

Her chin rested delicately on the heel of his palm like a precious egg. His other hand, fingers wet with her exertions, cupped her buttocks, both buttocks; she was that small. As she rode relentlessly up and down on his penis, Jerome continued to think about Fontana's monkey—he couldn't help it with Violette squatting over him, poised on her toes like a little creature waiting to spring from the massive limb of a gigantic rubber tree. She was bringing herself to orgasm, and went on working the helpless shaft, itself beginning to jerk involuntarily in its own death throes, until Jerome heard her distant cries echoing throughout the jungle.

1997

From HOBOKEN
Chapter 4

April 1977

The Stamford Arms wasn't a seriously bad place to live, but it was noisy and it was filthy. If you wanted *clean,* you had to clean it yourself. If you wanted quiet, you had to either shoot the motherfuckers or go out. Bootsy Holloway went out, although he would have preferred to shoot the scum that hung in the hallways downstairs fucking themselves up on smack and fizzy wine.

Since arriving in New York from the benighted coastal town of Belhaven, North Carolina in February, Bootsy had made only one friend. This was the janitor or *super,* as he liked to call himself, Percival Thomas Nolan, known as Tommy-Tom. This evening Tommy-Tom had invited Bootsy to go out to Hoboken for dinner. Tommy-Tom had also said they might take in the fair. He had said the fair sucked but that The Jewel, a bar nearby, had *topless* and the crowd was mixed. Anyone was allowed in as long as they didn't start any fights or, worse, piss on the floor. Bootsy was really looking forward to meeting Tommy-Tom's family too.

As Tommy-Tom, one hand on the wheel and one hand on the stick, piloted his Pontiac Bonneville expertly through the jammed-up traffic and down into the Lincoln Tunnel, Bootsy admired his new friend's lacquered do.

"Your hair always looks so nice," said Bootsy.

"I keep it that way." Tommy-Tom shook his head from side to side to demonstrate the holding power of the styling-gel he used.

"My Uncle Tookus, he's got hair like that," said Bootsy, patting his own, which was electric-cut, high on the crown. "But they say he's mostly white too, like—what's that mother's name?"

"Who?"

"That big-mouth nigger up in Harlem."

"How the fuck should I know?"

"Always says 'Keep the faith, baby.'"

"Oh, that mother."

"That's the man. Pretty."

"Yea. I bet he's got some nice snatch sittin on his face."

"I could eat some right now."

Tommy-Tom, the tiles in the tunnel reflected in his highway-patrolman sunglasses, stared curiously at Bootsy. To Bootsy, it looked like Tommy-Tom had a Chiclet factory inside his head.

"What's your wife's name again?" asked Bootsy.

"Val. Valerie."

"Oh yea, I remember now. It ain't none of my business, but she pretty?"

"For a white woman?"

"I ain't sayin that..." Bootsy laughed nervously.

"She's pretty as any of them. She used to have those nipples I like, until she had the kid."

"Them young black ones got the little puffy ones too."

"No shit?" Now Tommy-Tom laughed.

"No shit."

"I forgot to tell Val you're coming."

"She gonna blow?"

"I'll stop and get her a bottle."

"That's cool."

"I better call her. What the fuck—if she's in her bathrobe or something, she'll get pissed off."

"She like to look nice when y'all's got company."

"She likes to look nice when there's dick around." Tommy-Tom had to laugh at that too.

"What, even black dick?"

Tommy-Tom laughed even harder, and said, "Especially black dick." Then, "Only kidding." And rubbed his free hand over Bootsy's arm. "Nice suit."

Bootsy brightened. "I got it way downtown, near Wall Street. The label says *Cardin*."

"Yea, I've heard of that. Maybe I'll wear a suit tonight. Fuck it, let's just stop at The Jewel. I can call her from there."

"That's cool."

Bootsy liked The Jewel. He liked it so much that it made Tommy-Tom proud. Tommy-Tom called Val and told her they'd be home after a couple drinks. Then they'd go to the fair and have something to eat. He even agreed to have little Billy come along—it would be good for him to have firsthand experience of a grown black man. Val said, *Sure, that sounds nice, Tommy-Tom.* But she knew she and Billy would be alone together in front of the television for the rest of the evening. Later, after calling to ask if it was OK, she would send Billy down to Mr. Mainwaring's for another bottle of Seagram's.

Dr. Herbert's office was very bright and Diego Ildefonso was naked. He hadn't the strength, for the moment, to put his clothes back on. Dr. Herbert had gestured for him to, although he may have only been gesturing for him to sit down.

"You have a small tumescent growth just to the south of your bladder," explained Dr. Herbert. "That's what I kept poking at. I wouldn't worry though, these things often dissipate themselves. There's really no need at this stage for a biopsy."

Christian Herbert, as far as Diego was concerned, wasn't very like a doctor. He was more like a retired airline pilot. The sort of fellow who spends his declining years, without perceptibly declining, on the sunny fairways of an expensive country club somewhere in temperate America.

"Your weight, dear boy, has it increased?" asked Dr. Herbert.

"My complaint has nothing to do, I think, with..." But Diego hadn't the inclination to communicate his own awareness of his ridiculous size.

"Mustn't eat before one sleeps," joked Dr. Herbert.

Diego's indignation miraculously provided him with the energy to drag on his clothes. Balancing on one foot and then the other, he felt sufficiently distracted to pursue with Dr. Herbert the specific attributes of his horror. Dr. Herbert communicated no impatience whatsoever from his position by the room's only window. This was due to the fact that he wasn't actually listening to Diego but watching a young boy standing at the far end of the alleyway outside his office throwing a turtle high into the air, again and again, which fell, again and again, to strike the pavement. Eventually, Dr. Herbert turned from the window.

"Don't look so grave," he said, smiling by merely showing his teeth. "How about if we do both brain and body scans? St. Mary's has the gear..."

"I only have Saturday afternoons and Sundays off."

"We can do it in the evening. I'll have Linda call tomorrow morning and see how late they keep a technician on. Come to think of it, they have a special for poor folks on Wednesday evenings."

"Tomorrow? That would be OK, I guess. Do you mind calling me at the shop, rather than at home?"

Dr. Herbert glanced over the top of his desk, then sighed. "I'll make a mental note, how's that?"

"Do I owe you anything for today?" Diego realized this was a stupid question.

"Linda's left. I'll have her write it up in the morning." Dr. Herbert turned and gazed curiously at Diego. "Are you busy? I mean, right now?"

Diego didn't know what to say.

"Want to go for a drink? If you haven't heard already, Jane and I are splitting up. We'd always intended to, when the kids were old enough. You know, when they'd gone off to college. Well, Lance is at Swarthmore now and Judy's at Bryn Mawr..."

Diego figured he'd better say yes. It might help keep the bill down. "Mind if I give my wife a call? The telephone's through there, isn't it?"

When Dolores finally answered, he asked her how it had gone between Roland and Chief Huff. She said OK but wanted to discuss Roland's frame of mind with him later at length. He said, "Barbiche wants me to stick around and have a look at the leftover stuff from Milan."

"It won't sell," was her response.

Diego knew he'd taken the right approach. "I know," he said, "but it looks smart in the window."

When Dr. Herbert suggested he and Diego take a little exercise by walking over to the Lambeth Hotel on Fourth

Street, Diego asked if they couldn't take Dr. Herbert's car—he said his reluctance to walk had to do with a tendency to fatigue. Once they were in the car, he became much livelier and expressed an interest in a new drinking establishment in Weehawken, which was one place, as far as he knew, he and Dolores hadn't any friends or acquaintances. Instantly, he and Christian Herbert were headed in the direction of that useless town with its ghostly slope of dilapidated *villas* and dizzying view of the filthy mire that floats just beyond the opening to the Lincoln Tunnel.

Teddy Rozzo had taken the twins Margaret and Margery, and the bookish Theresa, to a special evening mass for their dead brother Mikie. Babs and Gus had stayed home with the baby, even though Theresa had thought this shameful and had expressed this opinion to her father. Gus had given Theresa five dollars not to go whining to her mother about it. Theresa had said she would make an offering of the five dollars to the church; it was a bribe, and therefore dirty money, which could, conceivably, be made clean by Jesus Christ. Gus had assured Theresa that this would be a commendable gesture. Theresa went away contented. Teddy had winked at his father over the girls' heads as he'd led them down the hallway and then out the front door.

"I think we'd better call Chief Huff," was the first thing Babs said when Gus entered their darkened bedroom. The baby lay sleeping against her hip.

Gus sat on the end of the bed facing their personal TV. As was usual now, due to the presence of the infant, there was picture but no sound. Groaning noisily with the effort, he pulled off his shoes without first untying them.

"I thought you said Val was going to talk to Tommy-Tom?"

"She couldn't get him."

Gus got up and went to the closet, pulling off his shirt and tossing it onto the dresser as he did. At the closet door he turned and dropped his trousers, then reached into his underpants and shifted his testicles from back to front.

"Do I *have* to wear pajamas?"

"When Dominic's in bed with us."

"Oh, for Christ's sake..." Gus kicked his trousers and his underpants into the closet and shut the door.

"Honey, what about air conditioning?"

"What about it?"

"Is it hot enough out?"

"It's not hot enough in here."

Babs rolled onto her side and moved the baby up to her breast. She did this because she knew it would annoy Gus, who would probably want to make love as soon as he got into bed.

"Oh man, don't start with Dominic. Alright?!"

"Why're you being so mean, Gus? Our little Mikie's dead and you're acting like I don't even have any feelings." Babs began to cry. "I have feelings. I have lots of feelings, otherwise I wouldn't of had all our beautiful children. Mikie was beautiful. All our children are beautiful. Look at little Dommie, honey. He's real beautiful too." The tears streamed over Babs's cheeks, and she clutched the baby tighter.

Gus came around the bed and sat by her, his elbow pressing down into the pillow on which he would eventually lay his head. He reached out and patted her hair where she had it bunched up and pinned at the back. It felt nice.

"You have pretty hair," he whispered.

"So what?"

"It's because I love you. I want you to be happy."

"How can I be happy when you're so mean?"

"I'm not trying to be mean."

"Well then, be nice." Babs wiped her eyes.

"We scared the fucking shit out of Freddie Friedrich today." Gus hoped this would brighten her up, but instead Babs turned serious, without acting sad.

"Freddie Jr.'s already been punished."

"By who?"

"By me."

"Slapping the kid don't mean squat."

"Teddy thinks we should talk to Chief Huff about it again."

"Yea, I know, Teddy's the big expert."

"I'll bet Tommy-Tom won't know where she is. He won't know anything."

"Wait a second. Didn't you call to ask her friends?"

"I called some after school. They don't know."

"Who'd you call?"

"You know, her friends."

"Like who, Rosalie?"

"And some others. Honey, look at Dommie, he's sucking while he's asleep."

"He's dreaming. Dogs and cats do the same thing."

Now, gazing down at the baby, Babs smiled. "Who knows but maybe Freddie Jr. did something with our Alicia. That could happen."

"OK, so I call Huff."

"Just as long as he don't have to come over." Again she was frowning.

"What?"

"I don't want him staring at me."

"What're you talking *staring?*"

"At the fair, he put his arm around me."

"You sound like fucking Alicia. It must be something in the women in this family, in *your* family."

"Jesus would hate you for saying that. I know when men are looking at me wrong."

Gus eased back against the velveteen plush of the padded headboard. "I just thought of something. Kidnapping's a federal offense. Remember? In that TV movie about Lindbergh— if you go over the state line it's federal."

"What state line?"

"Like if you go into New York or Pennsylvania, even by mistake, you can get the electric-chair."

"I didn't know they still had one." Babs tried to remember the film Gus was referring to but could only come up with an image of two guys, one white and one black, wearing cute hats and standing out in a field at night.

"I gotta sleep," said Gus. "There's Mikie's funeral tomorrow."

Staring at him, Babs lowered the bodice of her nightgown, so he could watch her suckle little Dominic. Eventually they both grew quiet.

Shirlee Simonaire, the topless dancer, had had polio as a child and her legs were too short. She was The Jewel's greatest attraction, aside from its dollar-cocktails at *Happy Hour*. It was well past *Happy Hour* when Bootsy scored the gram of coke from another brother out in the parking-lot. He and Tommy-Tom were about to go back outside to snort some when Chief Leon Huff entered the bar. He was looking for Tommy-Tom.

"Sorry," said Huff, "but your pal Gus sent me down here to speak with you. His call was relayed to me and I was in the neighborhood."

"When aren't you?" replied Tommy-Tom, grinning up at him drunkenly. "Oh, this is my bud Bootsy Holloway, from down south."

Huff nodded at Bootsy. "You remind me a little of Hound Dog Taylor, the Chicago bluesman."

"Thank you, sir," said Bootsy.

"I believe he just died," said Huff.

"He used to be dead in my mind too," said Bootsy.

"I got to talk to your man here," said Huff.

"My man," said Bootsy, and hugged Tommy-Tom, being careful not to touch his hair. Then, gazing up at Shirlee on the little stage covered in purple shag, Bootsy commented, "That damn thang is low to the ground."

"Give it a good sniff," said Tommy-Tom and rose from his seat to take a pee.

Huff followed Tommy-Tom into the Men's Room. By the time they stood side-by-side under the lavatory's single circular fluorescent tube, Tommy-Tom was in tears.

"I feel so bad," whimpered Tommy-Tom, taking out his penis.

"So do I," said Huff, taking out his.

"That kid was my godchild."

"Good place to drown your sorrow."

"I'm sad for Mikie. He had a good little arm. Little fucker could throw. I don't know where he got it—Gus throws like a girl."

"Maybe that's why they asked you to be Mikie's godfather."

"Yea. Probably."

"I'm actually here to inquire about Alicia." Huff laid his free hand on Tommy-Tom's shoulder, to keep him from leaving the facility.

Tommy-Tom stared down at the Chief's fingers. His nails were manicured and glistening with clear polish, and he wore a high school graduation ring, a police academy ring, and a large signet ring with the letters *LHR* engraved in black onyx.

"My girl," said Tommy-Tom. He gazed wistfully into the Chief's eyes. "She gave me a real nice present last Christmas."

"What was that?"

"An ashtray." Tommy-Tom, his tears suddenly a distant memory, was now smiling with irrepressible joy.

"An ashtray?"

"A joke one. Like with a girl with her thing available to put your cigarette in."

The Chief blushed. He shook his penis, replaced himself, and carefully pulled up his fly. "This kid is, what, fourteen years old?"

"Fucking kids are premature these days," said Tommy-Tom. He too withdrew from the urinal. "She wanted to go into the city. So I took her. I stopped at the Stamford, where I work —I don't know, man—she just wasn't in the fucking car when I got back."

As they made their way back to the bar, the Chief questioned Tommy-Tom further, but only just. "Anyone see you?"

"What, at the Stamford?"

The Chief nodded.

"How should I know?"

Huff didn't know what else to ask the scumbag so he excused himself, after attempting to note any identifying marks on the black man.

"Fucking police," said Tommy-Tom to Bootsy, "in Belfast they'd blow that fucking busybody-pig into the sea."

"I don't know nothin like that, man."

"You sound like me," sneered Tommy-Tom, "and I make myself fucking puke taking it up the ass from the likes of Huff."

"What's *Huff?*"

"That mother that was just harassing me. You want to do some of that stuff now? We can go into the john. Nobody'll bother us in there."

"I thought *he* was just botherin you in there?"

"Man, I took *him* in there. You wanna do some or not?"

"Hey man, what's mine is yours."

When they were in the Men's Room, noses turning to ice, Tommy-Tom had another bright idea. "Shirlee's one of my girls."

"One of y'all's *whats?*"

"She shows me a good time. She'd like you."

"Hey, hey," said Bootsy, feeling positive.

"She lives off Palisades Avenue over in Union City, only about ten minutes from here. She'll do us over there."

"We gotta pay her?"

"Give her some of your toot. She'll suck the fucking thing all night long."

"I ain't got all night long. Unless y'all gives me a ride back and I don't have to worry about gettin no taxi."

"No problem, my man," said Tommy-Tom.

Back at the bar, having ordered another Schlitz for himself and a White Russian for Bootsy, Tommy-Tom pointed his finger, the one he'd been exploring his numb nose with, at Shirlee. She smiled back from her perch by the stage, then returned to slowly sipping her rum and Coke.

"He's gonna want me to service his friend too," she said to Eliot, her favorite barman, a moment or two later.

"Spades think they're God's gift to women," remarked Eliot. Then, watching Tommy-Tom and Bootsy more carefully, added, "I'd rather fuck the black stud than the other guy."

"You know Tommy-Tom, El. He's always in here," said Shirlee. But to herself, she said, *I hope he doesn't want to use that fucking car antenna on me again.*

Diego Ildefonso approached his house. The joy he knew as he gazed up at his darkened windows was nearly boundless. His wife and child lay sleeping behind those grimy panes. The grime of winter, it would vanish with the wipe of a soft cloth and a little ammonia and water, the minutiae of Dolores's life. All around him, the city begged for deliverance. As the filthy mists drew about Diego Ildefonso, like the destitute hags who had confronted so many other great men, he heard the sirens of Hoboken singing. He heard the electrifying wail of the fire, and the somber thunder of the lowering doom.

Diego mounted the steps and stood before his front door. Where had he been until such an hour, not just looking at shoes? No, he was having a drink with Lou Nasserman, the sales rep from De Palma Roma. Mystifyingly, he again heard Dr. Herbert calling from his expensive car, as he had only moments before: *Don't kid yourself, Diego, we're all animals!* Dr. Herbert had been laughing. One day, like everyone else, Christian Herbert, the mere man, would watch helplessly as his own muscle turned to mush. Diego took little satisfaction in this. There was no consolation in knowing that the arrogant bastard would perish too.

Dolores recognized Diego's weight on the bed. It was gentle. He was with her, and she was grateful.

"Roland's alright," she said.

It was nearly midnight by the time Tommy-Tom and Bootsy made it over to Shirlee's apartment in Union City. Tommy-Tom had done too much of Bootsy's coke at The Jewel and had turned very pale on the drive over. His face was riveting with cold sweat and he had an aching under his jaw which felt like it began somewhere in his left arm. Bootsy, on the other hand, was riding high on just the right combination of cocaine and vodka.

Shirlee had left The Jewel at eleven so she would have time to freshen up before the boys arrived. When she had company she initially pleased herself by playing the music she liked, knowing her guests would have their own ideas once things got started. She was most fond of Motown, and especially The Supremes. She figured Bootsy would appreciate the fact that a youngish white woman had such a fondness for the material that constituted the biggest success black entertainers had had in her life-time; he did not look like the type who liked jazz. Shirlee had decided to wear a slinky sarong for the occasion. The sarong was maneuverable and looked good, even though it had been relatively inexpensive, a worthwhile consideration in case Tommy-Tom got into the rough stuff and the garment was damaged or destroyed. On top, she wore a form-fitting lycra halter that made it appear that her breasts were much larger and firmer than they were. She never let anyone near her breasts. Well, there had been one boy, but he'd been young enough not to want to manipulate her roughly; he'd wanted only to fondle, caress, and, most touching of all, suckle her. Shirlee was tidying the kitchen when the buzzer sounded, signalling guests in the horrible over-lit cubicle her landlord referred to as *the lobby*.

"Hi Tommy-Tom," said Shirlee, opening the door without taking the usual precautions.

"He don't look so good," said Bootsy.

"Maybe I better lie down," said Tommy-Tom, "where it's quiet."

Shirlee led him into her sewing-room, rather than the bedroom. Laid in rows across what she referred to as the "baby bed" was her collection of Barbie Dolls.

"What the fuck?" said Tommy-Tom.

For an anguishing moment, Shirlee thought he going to throw himself onto the bed, which would have meant hours and hours of checking for snapped joints and torn seams. Thankfully, he went to the mirror that hung over the dresser instead.

"I got blood in my nose hairs."

As Shirlee quickly removed the Barbie Dolls, she wondered if Tommy-Tom was going to be good for anything: she hated the idea of having to suck his limp dick for hours, while he got drunker and drunker or, worse, more and more embarrassed. It didn't matter what anyone paid her, it just wasn't any fun.

Tommy-Tom lay down and Shirlee made a big fuss of seeing that he was comfortable before returning to the living-room and Bootsy.

"My man ain't used to that shit," said Bootsy. He was sitting stiffly on the sofa with one leg curled under him and the other stretched out, his foot resting on a pile of Vogue magazines.

"He'll be alright. In a little while maybe we'll fix him another drink. Sometimes that helps."

"I could use one myself."

"Me too. What would you like?"

"Anything with vodka—soda, juice, even milk's OK."

Shirlee was very much aware of Bootsy watching her through the doorway to the kitchen as she took down the bottle of vodka and went to the fridge. It felt good to have someone new checking her out. "I don't see Tommy-Tom that often."

"You'd have to be Mrs. James Bond or something to put up with that shit."

Shirlee thought she knew what he meant. "Well, Mr. Bond's on vacation now."

"The man never stops. He just works all day and party's all night."

"Oh? You want a slice of anything in with the ginger ale? I have a brand new orange—"

"Just an extra-big slice of vodka."

He's cute, thought Shirlee. "That's a wonderful suit."

There was a moment of quiet before the next record landed on the turntable and the needle hopped into the groove. Shirlee heard Bootsy say to himself, "Maybe I better do some lickin of my own before the man gets up." Then, over the introduction to the song, she heard Tommy-Tom.

"I go first."

"Sure, sure, my man," Bootsy replied.

Just as Shirlee was putting the ginger ale back in the fridge, she felt Tommy-Tom standing behind her in the doorway.

"I'll bet you'd like one too," she said, without turning. She dreaded the look on Tommy-Tom's face in the harsh light of the kitchen. "You two get comfortable and I'll be right in."

"Do it," said Tommy-Tom.

When Shirlee brought the drinks in on a tray, her Mexican one with huge colorful blossoms scattered gaily over a black background, she found Tommy-Tom was now sitting on the sofa while Bootsy had been displaced to the tiny settee by the hallway door. It struck Shirlee that Bootsy was actually quite handsome, his dark head set off against the pink wallpaper, covered all-over in minty green bows. Tommy-Tom had taken his dick out and laid it, like a big cold noodle, over the cloth of his trousers. Tommy-Tom wore those trousers with the tab and metal fasteners, rather than a belt. They made him look like a smart-ass hippie from the waist down. Shirlee set the tray on the carpet by Tommy-Tom's feet. She then knelt by him and offered him his drink.

"Hey, you'd make a good wife," he said. "Wouldn't she, Bootsy?"

Bootsy only stared.

"Take Bootsy his drink."

She did, on her knees.

"Thanks," said Bootsy.

"Now, you have yours," said Tommy-Tom. "But show us your ass while you drink it."

She swivelled around—somewhat shyly, it seemed to Bootsy—and raised the sarong at the back. She sipped her drink while balanced that way on one hand. Shirlee glanced over at Bootsy. She could tell he was getting excited. Her panties had ruffles joined to the elastic, now creasing the cheeks of her bottom, and she knew it looked nice.

"Stick your finger in there," said Tommy-Tom. "Not you. Bootsy."

"Please don't," Shirlee whispered to Bootsy. "I don't want you to."

"Finish your drink and shut up," said Tommy-Tom.

Shirlee could hear the unmistakable sound of Tommy-Tom playing with himself. His mouth always made a noise like he was sucking an ice-cube.

"Man, I just wanna watch. I'm enjoyin my drink," said Bootsy. But his drink only hung loosely in his hand. Shirlee worried he might spill it on the carpet.

"Don't you want me to suck Bootsy while *you* watch?" she asked Tommy-Tom, her head cocked fetchingly over her shoulder. She could feel her lips numbing with the vodka. "Don't you?"

"Put her face on the cushion, and give it to her that way," said Tommy-Tom, but Bootsy remained, slightly listing, where he sat. "What's the matter, man?"

"Maybe he doesn't like doggy-fashion," said Shirlee.

"I do," said Bootsy. "But I ain't in the mood yet."

"What a fucking bunch of babies." Tommy-Tom pushed off the sofa, down onto the carpet, taking his drink with him. He came up behind Shirlee.

Shirlee jerked to one side, but Tommy-Tom grabbed her. His glass landed somewhere between there and the kitchen, his drink soaking the carpet. Bootsy watched as Tommy-Tom yanked down Shirlee's underpants, licked his thumb and stuck it in her butt. Tommy-Tom then tried to force his dick into her pussy using his other hand, while keeping her in place with the pressure of his thumb.

"Your nail!" screeched Shirlee.

"Should I stick it in here?" demanded Tommy-Tom.

"OK, OK, just stop hurting me," begged Shirlee.

Tommy-Tom savored the moment.

"She always acts like this," Tommy-Tom told Bootsy. "It works every time...*what the fuck?!*"

Suddenly Shirlee was on her back in the middle of the room and Tommy-Tom was on top of her.

"You fucking cocksucking faggot!" he shouted, grabbing Shirlee between the legs. "Look at this shit—" he shouted at Bootsy. "Go get a fucking knife! In the kitchen!"

"You're *hurting* her," said Bootsy, standing over Tommy-Tom. "Don't be doin that, man."

But Tommy-Tom wouldn't stop. Bootsy could sense the desperation rising in Shirlee's limbs. Ramming his forehead into her throat, Tommy-Tom brought the entire weight of his body down on her. Bootsy tried pulling at his head, but Tommy-Tom was too close to the floor, his weight centered too low. Bootsy's long fingers circled Tommy-Tom's neck. He dug his nails into the flesh, trying to bring Tommy-Tom to his senses. Nothing happened. Bootsy scooped up the empty glass lying on the carpet and smashed it against the side of Tommy-Tom's head. Tommy-Tom reared back and stared at the ceiling. Down came Tommy-Tom's head again like a hammer, breaking Shirlee's nose, snapping off her two front teeth. Bootsy took the bottom of the glass, now covered in his own blood, clutched up Tommy-Tom's chin and dug into the flesh of his throat. This time Tommy-Tom's head fell with the full weight of his consciousness. Shirlee watched as he came in childlike spasms to lie beside her. His blood spread quickly into the carpet. The thick pile drank it up. Bootsy bolted, leaving the door to 3B standing open.

1999

POETRY

128

MY CASUAL HEART
On Religion

Fires burning to keep
the howling cold at bay,
St. Stephen's Day
draws to a close.
We assume the posture
of the drowsy
double-backed beast.
Yes, we shall hibernate
until the sun
creeps over the equator
and the skin
loosens pleasantly
with the promise
of nature's heat.

On the Day we drank
to your savage gods
but now we cower
at the thought
of their return.
May they never more,
especially in celebration,
be manifest
in my casual heart,
but together let us
only watch
as they come perpetually
to inhabit the countless
inelegant bodies
of the others
who writhe with dread
content.

Thankfully,
the gifts are all dispersed
and the eating
less mordantly abundant,
as now we retire
with the evening shadows
and so very,
very sweetly are embraced
by nothing more
ominous than sleep.

28.12.01

AS THE HEAVENS FALL
On 9/11

As the heavens fall,
so too falls the hour.
The drafts of a thousand
empty rooms
dance over the streets,
then retreat.

Out of the fiery crease
they emerge,
seeking refuge from a storm
they cannot name,
while on their lips
trembles
the Word of God.

Nearer the sun,
others abandon themselves
into the light—
to fill their despairing souls
with the uplifting breath

of eternity.
And, as they fall,
delicate leaves
from silver birches,
we wonder.
From our balconies
we watch and
grow quieter still,
for now the wind,
once fragrant
with the scent
of the World's glory
and its decay,
blows through
our hearts too.

Like the desiccated moss
that once adorned
the weary flanks
of Brother Tommaso's tomb,
the weakening fibre of hope
shimmers with
the sun's healing rays
and turns to dust.

Today we weep
for the unnamed joy.

1/2.1.02

ZARIFE'S RELEASE
On the Consequences of War

Zarife ran in terror across the square on Al Mansour Melia, all
of Baghdad beside him. Stumbling, his knees split open, one
then the other, like brown eggs. He hid, cloaked in blood.

Sprinkled over his cheeks were droplets warm as tea, slick strands of scalp ribboned and unravelling in his hair. In the market place, his mother fell too, and his father, scurrying out from under the exhausted weight of the Bank of Rasheed's proscenium: masonry fused to naked feet, their flesh was cleaved, fragments of metal penetrating marrow like marmalade. Zarife felt their shadows fall, like lead, somewhere behind him.

Zarife awoke with tears staining his sleeves. He returned to sleep, following the path he and his wife Fareeza had taken over the blackened plain, Al Basrah a ghostly maze below. They had found the empty lane magnetic. Behind them lay the boiling Gulf, ahead of them the hills, lathered a silky gray by the breath of the inferno, its vapors lingering still in the acacias' dense filigree. In Fareeza's eyes, Zarife saw a sadness unlike any he had seen before. Taking her hand, he walked on, into the dusk. They would return home, carefully retracing their steps, all the way down to the sea.

They watched as their shadows, merging silently before them, slipped under the perilous weight of the evening light into the ash at their feet, and then she fell. Subterranean pipes burst with the heat, the earth yawned obliquely and into the void Fareeza plummeted, like a doll flung down by a petulant child. She sank rigidly upright, her body feeding the chasm of smoldering oil. The indigo hair burst into flames, the white hands fluttered upwards, the mouth he so adored blossomed and was lost in a burst of cinder.

Nothing—no ironical manifestation of optimism—could obscure the shame he felt each time Fareeza's imploring eyes sought his. The harbour lay before him, the horizon radiantly draped in cloud, empty even of a pitying glance. This dreaded theatre would forever be Zarife's nocturnal domain. As a melancholy child plays, so too he would play at nothing. Reaching out, as if his hands could hear, Zarife would find silence. The place he shared with Fareeza, so pure and fragile and utterly excruciating, would never be revealed, never obliterated. He often imagined sitting with his wife in the shade of a favourite palm on the terraces of Babylon Oberal, the serenity of their union bringing waves of calm to enfold him, his eyes weary of human commerce, legs aching with the diligence of his work. The earth was made of wandering sands, or so Zarife had thought, until from the depths of the desert's silence had shone its dark treasure, infernal liquid. Oil.

By the Tigres, at Al Amarah, Fareeza stood again in her parents' garden watching Zarife as he slept amongst the scented bells, her soul reaching down to possess his, vines cascading from limbs of carob. She patiently waited for him to awaken and observe the evening with loving eyes, the sun's waning brilliance concentrated in the wealth of her bosom. The light—her light—came shimmering through the gently rocking stems, muted colour held aloft, fuming, as she went singing into him, no vessel of ash. There would be no withering with age for Zarife either. The scourge of brutal modernity that had rendered his world obsolete had summoned him to the instruction of stealth and cunning. Men who failed to retaliate, he now knew, were men whose lives were merely straw to burn. One day, evincing no pity or restraint, he would realize the glory, and the horror, of immortality wrung from a life too meagre to disrespect. He would have no children.

Dawn came scudding over the walls of his bedroom, as Fareeza solemnly rode him, the colour hastening to his cheeks, into the light of a new day. With the act of love came awakening, and, paradoxically, despair. Fareeza had always done her best to sustain the intimacy shared so tenderly, steadfastly refusing to indulge her husband's darkness. Now Zarife knew what toll he must exact from the tyrants—not moral men, but greedy men without the stature of a sanctioned executioner—whose false indignation so damned them. These were the men who had annihilated his loved ones. Cowards of bleak technology, they would lie down, gasping for breath, with infamy. They would die drowning in the hubris of their own gluttony. His solitary

path would be uninterrupted, as he went humbly in pursuit of
his destiny. Over the temple rose the fires of oblivion, lighting
the way from his window, through a limitless network of air-
ways, into the comforting arms of Allah.

8/13.2.03

DREADED CITY
War in the Streets of Baghdad

I.

As a city grows, like a wild fungus
in the mind, it also spirals into pockets
of the ether, reaches up to haul down
the stars, and drive them into man's
nocturnal repositories—bars and discos,
cinemas, cafeterias, living-rooms, even
churches—for cities are beyond the
imagination, beyond the confines of
military strategy and its contingencies.
No army can penetrate the city's psyche,
neither can any mortal force destroy it;
the myriad souls who comprise its fabric
do not question the motives of the intruder,
for they instinctively know he has come
to violate and undo, to at least humiliate.

Those who, day after day, walk its streets,
smell its seasons changing, survive amidst
the city's complex of prejudices, accepting
the selfless inevitability of compromise,
reject and deny the invaders' alien logic.
These, the conqueror thinks, are the sorry,
uncivilized souls who have been waiting
to be embraced by my wealth, wanting

merely to walk shoulder-to-shoulder with
our legions, beneficent liberators all.
But the city waits to pop this fantasy
hungrily into its mouth, like a fat grape.

II.

His house blown to bits, wife and
children dead, a man is determined
to punish, at any cost, those
responsible. Out of the shattered
doorway emerges his ghastly
spectre, no onslaught equal to his
appetite for revenge. The streets
in which he played as a child are
now a jungle of fractured memories.

The soldier, trapped in a maze
of indecipherable signage,
corridors of shadow and light
signifying his mortality, hears
his brain stammer: lost but for
my weapon. How far the conqueror
travels, each city a wedding cake
on the horizon, a hornets' nest
fallen from a limb of purple cloud.

For the invader, there is nothing
more satisfying than marching
triumphantly along the enemy's
boulevards, and nothing more
anguishing for a city's people
to behold. The dance of liberation
is one without artifice, essential to
the resurrection of heartache.

Missiles ripping through steel
and concrete, shrapnel shattering
windows, penetrating flimsy
bathroom walls, abject fear
pervades the subconscious
to harvest depression and
psychosis, often eternally so.

Out of the desert mists, the tanks
lumber in, buildings reduced to
rubble. No semblance of a society
remains to hold aloft courageous
thoughts unfolding, only bitterness
driving ingenuity meagrely into
each darkened crevice. Women
eventually appear, wanting for sanity.

The older men imprisoned or dead,
boys barely in their teens are left
to face the occupying forces.
For years to come, these young men
will scrub clean their streets with
the blood of unsuspecting soldiers.
And the memory of each dead
soldier's friendly disposition and
unseemly largesse will bring a smile
to brighten each young man's face.

24/28.3.03

BEHIND THE VENETIAN BLINDS
Three Poems On Despair

CREATURES IN THE STREET

Shingles fall from his brow,
roof that covers the world.
Raising himself from his bed,
demanding nothing but sleep,
and still it goes on, the sorrow.
The creatures in the street,
who live without solace,
are harbouring within him,
awake or asleep, although
it very seldom gets that good.
And his mind knows no quiet,
but it is nothing as compared to—
a heartfelt round of applause,
because he can't now recall
how his kindness shone, and
it's time to stop remembering.
Send me all those leftover
flowers, he says, from all those
things that were cancelled,
all those things that had to do
with sadness, with celebration,
with any kind of love whatsoever.
Just, please, send them to me
because I've got room here.

LIKE A MOCKINGBIRD

She dances along not thinking
that she might fall down, down.
Oh my breasts, they'll keep me
afloat, she murmurs, and she

knows she looks so very good.
Where's my mom tonight?—
she frowns, knowing that she's
dead, and old Ralph, the bastard,
he's singing somewhere high up
in his tree like a mockingbird.
And still, how I loved him so,
because he brought the big love
into my room without anything
but tenderness, and never said
nothing bad about me or my
mom, no not never, and I
won't be like her, no not never.
I wouldn't let a fucker like
him get away with so much
money and good looks too.

NOT BREATHING

Somewhere just this side of
dawn, he wakes up not breathing,
looks at the clock and thinks:
now, I've finally done something
without trying, without anyone
telling me to hurry up, or to wait,
while I take my time not getting
there, and it was easy as cream pie.
Remember how every day or so
a shadow would cross your path?—
he asks himself, knowing no
shadow ever did, or spoke
to him, or showed him the way
down to the river where
everyone else makes love,
where everyone else finds
something to do that they
can't do in the light of day.

Except stop breathing, which
is now his strength, his pride,
award-winning as it isn't but
then, sudden as toast, he
gasps, taking in the air, and
it's all over, all that sweet
exclusivity is gone, and he's
walking along the dark river,
watching, after not working.

17.10.03 – for Mel Gooding

ON FIRST ENCOUNTERING ARTAUD

Ilona S. lived in a small non-descript apartment building which stood incongruously at the centre of a long tree-shrouded street of rather grand early American houses. She spoke with a light Polish accent, wore her long dark hair bound tightly to her head, and radiated the kind of quiet excitement that sensually inclined intellectuals sometimes do. It was a rainy autumn evening and I was to meet Ilona at her flat at eight o'clock. That was all there was to it. I had never been with her before and I can't now recall what had transpired that had led to this meeting. She welcomed me without ceremony, her hair wet with rain, and suggested I relax while she took a shower. The flat consisted of one big room with an alcove at the front over-looking the street, its windows heavily draped, in which stood the bed, which was high, a bath behind the chimney-breast at the other end, and a stove positioned awkwardly against the outside wall down from a tall glowering window on the alley-way. Against the other wall, not far from the door onto the common hallway, was a chest of drawers. It was this chest of drawers that finally had my full attention.

I decided to wait for Ilona to return from her shower situated comfortably on her bed. As my eyes strayed over the top of the big bureau, I became more and more curious about the various objects stationed there. What would a 22 year-old—she was four years older than I was—art student from Lodz keep on the ready? Naturally, I left the bed and crossed the room. When encountered, all of these intimate things, fascinating though they may have been, faded from view as my eyes fell upon the image of the attenuated Antonin Artaud. Immediately, I was fixed on Artaud's profile, petulant and somehow atrocious, as it fastened this paperback book to the top of the chest of drawers, but to no time or place. Examining the volume more closely, I found that Lawrence Ferlinghetti, whose City Lights Books I knew, had published this anthology (John Hirschman's *Artaud Anthology*) of Artaud's writing. There were more stark black and white images inside, all of which, along with the eruptive language—caca, peepee, jiji-creecree—thrilled me to the depths of my neurotic being. This book would be, I instantly understood, a limitlessly enriching source of disorientation and mystery. Artaud's disfigured goodness had acted upon me. When Ilona appeared from the bath, I asked her if I could borrow the book. With a knowing smile, and without selfishness, she said yes.

8.9.02 – for Stephen Barber

YOUR OLD FRIEND LOCOID
Side Effects of Corticosteroids

3rd July 2004

Jane Purcell*
Purcell Partnership
St. Agnes Road
Faversham
Kent BH8 3NJ
Dear June

Re Charles Nichol & Locoid

Psoriasis Topical Treatments: Side effects of corticosteroids are extremely rare but may include high blood pressure, infections, cataracts, glaucoma, diabetes, psychosis, and osteoporosis. *RealAge.com*

As you know, Roger** has discovered that the cream — Locoid—Charles has been rubbing into himself since the age of 16 for his psoriasis can cause Hypothalamic-pituitary-adrenalin axis suppression. I spent most of Friday afternoon doing research on the internet for Roger and found that HPA axis suppression does seem to lead directly to suppression of emotion—i.e. not vocalizing one's anguish, desperation, etc.—but can conversely engender a propensity for impulsive violence, especially in couples. *Psychosis*. I also learned that post-traumatic stress syndrome triggered in childhood by abandonment by the parent—mother rats lick their young when they are disorientated to generate reassuring brain chemicals—which amounts to abuse through alienation, is often accompanied by a cortisol response that leads to a stress threshold in later life that can, in rare cases, be aggravated by HPA axis suppression brought about by prolonged use of corti-costeroids like Locoid. Charles may very well have crossed his threshold in the garden at 71 Arlington Square on the morning of 3rd May. It does seem rather plausible, seeing as Charles is such a gentle soul. Locoid also causes high blood sugar which, anyone familiar with alcohol abuse knows, can cause sudden eruptions of physical violence.

Kind regards
Marcus

*Jane Purcell – Solicitor
** Roger Bennison – Barrister

3.7.04

AND THE YEARS SAIL INSEPARABLE
Writing in Prison

This here is an open letter to everybody and everything
that has been mistreating me since my day of birth.
I was mistaken when I promised to try and understand.
If you think my memory is lame then you can keep
the evil lies of that evil world you like to call your own.
Nothing is forgot and nobody goes without being seen.
I give up writing love letters, and romance. Rose knows
the way back to the rain being the tears in your baby's eyes,
but I figure it's like feeling restless in the middle of nowhere,
and nobody's watching or waiting for you, no not ever.
    Paradise, take this child lost in the flood.

So I went out that night to do my dance up and down the block.
The trees were like cliffs of despair. Lovers kissed by the sea
beneath the moon, their torn tree burning to disgrace the sky.
I remember summer honeysuckle, two people dancing on a
veranda, and I followed the black whispering river through
the flesh I would never away. There was nothing to be afraid
of, and the voice of night said to me: the years sail inseparable.
I had heard in the darkness lovers tell of life loving death and
death loving life. But I was like a child growing grey waiting
for the rain to wash away—younger among valleys of lead, the
remaining become the dead. So I murdered the tender ones as
fearless morning broke the night in two. Her mistaken body
and his misshapen life come to meet their end in a deserted
street.
    Paradise, take these children lost in the flood.

1970

A BOY AND HIS BULLET
Draft of Film Concept by Jim Nash

SCENE 1

(B&W) Winter, 1962. A chilly classroom in the Margate
School of Art Buildings. The lesson in progress is mathemat-
ics. Felix Jacobowski, aged 12—denim jacket and jeans, copper
rivets around the pockets, striped shirt, chrome-studded belt,
black winkle pickers, and a DA haircut a la James Dean—is
not a model pupil. He has never been particularly interested in
maths, although he knows he is quite capable of doing well in
this subject. His tutor, with his bland late 1940's style double-
breasted suit, Brylcreamed hair, and scientist's glasses, is a
boring fart.

As the tutor drones on, Felix scratches around his pine desk top
with his penknife which he always carries with him, along with
a packet of five Woodbines and a smelly petrol lighter. Felix
wins the Woodbines on the pinball machines in the arcades on
the Margate seafront during his lunchbreak. All of the desk
tops are littered with graffiti—cartoons, jokes, girls' names,
etc.—but there is one particular mark on Felix's desk top which
captures his interest. It is dark and round and hovers just below
the surface. Eventually, Felix excavates the object, a bullet
head. The slug has one flattened end, which apparently occurred when the plank of timber was sawn at the mill. As Felix
examines the bullet more closely, his imagination transfixes
him and he embarks on a journey to the spot where the projec-
tile had conceivably first entered the pine tree.

SCENE 2

It is a freezing cold afternoon, the year 1943. Somewhere in
Poland, a massive pine forest cloaked in snow, and a small
clearing at its centre. A bedraggled figure, face gaunt but filled

with dignity, is tied to a huge pine. There is bruising about the man's forehead. His clothes are in tatters. The man is trembling with fear. Behind him stands an army truck with a tarpaulin cover, while ahead of him stand seven German soldiers. Six of the soldiers are regulars, while the seventh is an officer in jackboots and jodhpurs. The officer gives the order to aim. The forest is silent, the boughs of the trees heavy with snow. The order to fire, which echoes for what seems an interminable moment, is suddenly drowned in rifle fire. The man bound to the tree gazes heavenward. (Colour) Blood gushes from his chest and spatters the snow at his feet. The man slumps forward, his torment over. The officer examines the body, cuts the prisoner free. The man sinks to the ground. One bullet, having torn completely through him, remains lodged in the tree. The soldiers shuffle through the snow and climb into the truck. The engine roars into life, exhaust steaming out over the white drifts, and the truck trundles off into the distance. The forest is quiet once more, the dead man's fragile features starkly beautiful.

16.1.00

MAGNUM DICTUM
The Viceroy's Siesta

Yes, my
id is a pid
in a pod,
that's me.

My magnum dictum,
like the accountant's
brief,
cloisters the thief,
as his id from its piddling
pod

descends to rivulet
the welcoming palms
of Misfortune
and her sister, Ilene.

Of vinegar and
saccharine
the two sing,
also occasionally:

How blue, how blue
the sea does shine
in our beguiling eyes,
as its vagrant mists
play upon our breasts,
yielding but resilient,
and we effortlessly
shift our dappled limbs
into position.

Assault he must
the towering precipice
of his lobster salad
and digest before
commencing further.

In the afternoon,
Misfortune and Ilene
casually make use
of his rumoured
stamina, shredded
but not shaken.

After, he watches
Ilene in repose,
modest restraints
and musty drapes
of the confessional

eschewed,
while Misfortune
too reclines,
vertically behind
the diamond light
of the shower curtain,
his thirst momentarily
subdued
by Boticelli's palette.

And so, amidst his slumbers,
his pid once again alights
upon one tousled head still wet,
not Misfortune's but her sister's,
in a world without split-ends,
amen.

2.9.02

Publishing Sources

Displaced Person
The Anxiety of Siron Franco – 3am Magazine and Zinos Review
Cities of the World – Newtopia Magazine
Beyond Fahrenheit 9/11 – Democratic Underground
Drown in My Own Tears – The Raw Story
The Dead Inherit the Breeze – Newtopia Magazine
Lucian Freud – *Blunt Edge 5*: Journal of the Peter Fuller Foundation
You Are Very Kind, I Said – Tartan Films DVD Booklet and State of Art Magazine
Breton Shoots Self in Penis – *The Whistler*: Journal of the Chelsea Arts Club and Newtopia Magazine
General Rules of the School of Abject Expressionism – *Blunt Edge 4*: Journal of the Peter Fuller Foundation
Conversation from the Margins
Verdon Angster – Burnhill Wolf Books
The Miracle of Fontana's Monkey – Burnhill Wolf Books and 3am Magazine
Hoboken – 3am Magazine
My Casual Heart – Newtopia Magazine
As the Heavens Fall – Newtopia Magazine
Zarife's Release – Newtopia Magazine
Dreaded City – Newtopia Magazine and Zinos Review
Behind the Venetian Blinds – written for Mel Gooding
On First Encountering Artaud – written for Stephen Barber
Your Old Friend Locoid
And the Years Sail Inseparable
A Boy and His Bullet – written for Jim Nash
Magnum Dictum – Newtopia Magazine

Internet Journals: 3am Magazine, Democratic Underground, Newtopia Magazine, The Raw Story, and Zinos Review